SKEET SHOOTING WITH D. LEE BRAUN

D1028247

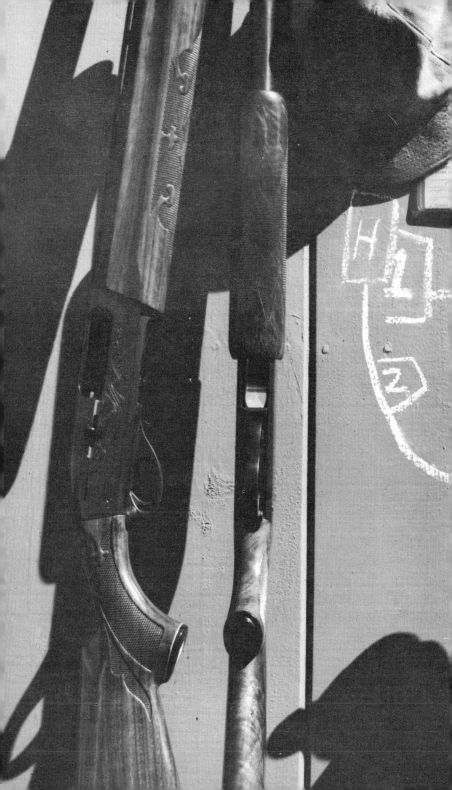

SKEET SHOOTING WITH D. LEE BRAUN

A WORLD CHAMPION SHOWS HOW SKEET CAN MAKE YOU A BETTER FIELD SHOT

EDITED BY ROBERT CAMPBELL

A BENJAMIN COMPANY/RUTLEDGE BOOK

Photo Credits

*Bert and Richard Morgan Studio:
front cover, title page
Principles of Skeet, Stations,
In the Field, pgs. 99
top, and 111
Robert Stahman: back cover,
end sheets, In the Field,
with the exception of pgs. 99
top, and 111
Larry Madison Productions, Inc.:
camera gun sequences
D. Lee Braun: all others
Many of the instructional
photos in this book were taken
at the Palm Beach Gun Club,
Florida, through the cooperation
of its officers and members.*

CONTENTS

7

This book is the result of over thirty years'
shooting experience—experience to which many people
have contributed. I would like to express my regard for these
friends, for without their encouragement I might never
have fulfilled my desire to perfect my own shooting game.
Nor would I be at a point now where I feel I have
something to offer a new generation of shooters.
First, then, this book is dedicated to my mother and father,
Elonia Braun Franklin and William Lee Braun. They brought me
into the world and gave me a chance to enjoy many
of the opportunities it affords. Next is Col. J. W. Speight
of Dallas, who took me on my first round of skeet and
thereby lit the fuse that gave me the impetus
to shoot as well as I have. I am also indebted to him for
my wife, Marian Speight Braun, whose much-appreciated
patience and encouragement have continually supported me in
my endeavor. Then comes an old boss—and an old friend—
Dewey Godfrey of Remington Arms, who made it possible for me to
progress with my shooting and who, incidentally, at times left
a few extra shells around that I could carry off and use for practice.
Two companions of my early shooting days, Felix S. "Red"
Hawkins and Roy Cherry, of Dallas, taught me to shoot
under pressure by their continual harassment and goading. And I
will be ever grateful to Grant Ilseng, of Houston, for instilling
in me high standards and principles of shooting
and a real understanding and enjoyment of this game.
I would like to extend my warmest regards to the many
personal friends I have made in the shooting fraternity, and to
say to new shooters: there's no better fraternity in the
world that you could join. Lastly, I would like to tip my tattered
shooting cap to the really fine company I have worked for
these last thirty-two years—Remington Arms, a company
that has made both my vocation and my avocation pleasurable and
afforded me many hours of happiness in this world.

SKEET SHOOTING WITH D. LEE BRAUN

HOW IT ALL BEGAN

BY ROBERT CAMPBELL

■ The sport of skeet shooting as we know it today started just about half a century ago on the grounds of the Glen Rock Kennels at Andover, Massachusetts. The kennels were owned by the late Charles E. Davies, a retired Boston businessman. An avid upland game hunter and a crack shot, Charles Davies was also a perfectionist who went to lengths unheard-of in those days in trying to improve his accuracy with a shotgun. He had two handy assistants—his son Henry and Henry's friend, Bill Foster.

Henry and Bill were boyhood companions in those years between 1910 and 1915, and spent a good deal of time grouse-hunting. In exchange for this privilege, the elder Davies pressed the boys into service from time to time to help him improve his shooting. Frequently, on missing a shot in the field, he would have them set up the old ''Expert'' trap, which was kept bolted to a plank; then he would position himself as he had been for the bird he missed. While the boys threw targets for him, Mr. Davies would fire away until he was smoking them one after another. In time, all three of them had a habit of correcting shooting faults with clay targets.

One winter evening around 1915, while sitting at the dinner table, the two Davieses got into a discussion about how to systematize this idea of shooting at targets from different positions so that

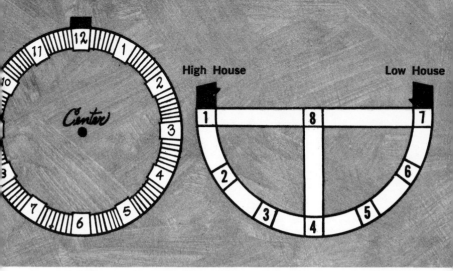

Original field was a clock design and had trap at Station 12 throwing targets toward 6. Modern field with trap at each end gives same effect.

each shooter would have exactly the same chance at each target. The result was a design for a shooting field, which they showed to Bill Foster the next day. The design was laid on the kennel grounds, and consisted of a circle with a twenty-five-yard radius that had twelve positions marked on the circumference, like the numbers on the face of a clock. The trap was staked down at 12 o'clock and positioned so it would throw clay targets toward 6. Starting at the 12 o'clock position, each shooter fired two shots from each of the twelve stations. Then he walked to the center of the circle with the single shell left over from his original box of twenty-five, and shot this close-range, incoming target. For the next few years this sport was avidly practiced by the threesome, who had dubbed it ''shooting around the clock,'' and they worked at it hard in the fall as practice for the hunting season.

Gradually the three shooters became aware of a defect in their scheme. Occasionally a target would pass right through the shot charge without being hit, indicating that the shot had scattered too widely by the time it reached the target. The radius of their circle was a little too large, putting these targets a bit out of range. So, in 1923, they reduced the radius to twenty yards to prevent such misses and the complaints and suspicions that no doubt sometimes **11**

Pacific Rod and Gun Club in San Francisco in 1939 during the first western national shoot. Note Pat Laursen's ready position under old rules.

arose as a result of these flukes—or supposed flukes.

For safety, the "clock" field required about 500 yards square of terrain to accommodate pellets fired in all directions. That was fine—until Mr. Davies' neighbor, John Hall, decided to go into the chicken business. As a result, a village of white hen houses cropped up in clear view of stations 7 to 11, and half the circle had to be abandoned. Bill Foster solved this problem by setting up a second trap at 6 o'clock. At the same time the stations were renumbered, so that 6 became 1, 12 became 7, and so on for the stations in between, the midfield station being numbered 8. With this arrangement, the same target angles were provided by the semicircle that the whole clock had previously afforded. Here were the basic elements of a modern skeet field, including the dimensions.

Both the clock and the later half-clock were providing the threesome with excellent field practice, for they were getting shots from all the angles—straightaways, crossing shots and incomers, with targets thrown from both right to left and left to right. But slowly they grew aware that there was one field shot their design didn't provide for. This was a bird flying across fifteen feet or more above the ground, a shot that appears to be going slowly **12** downhill as the shooter prepares to fire. Here the targets were *not* duplicating the field situation, because both traps were at ground level and the targets were shot while still on the rise. To compensate for this situation, Henry Davies and Bill Foster built an elevated structure for the trap at Station 1. The "structure" was an elm trunk about fifteen feet high with the trap fixed atop it.

Bill Foster, by now an editor and outdoor writer with *National Sportsman,* decided to share the field idea with the shooting public at large. The announcement appeared in 1926, both in the *Sportsman* and in *Hunting and Fishing,* along with a contest that featured a $100 cash prize for the best name for the new game. Mrs. Gertrude Hurlbutt of Dayton, Montana, walked off with the prize for her suggestion, "skeet," an old Scandinavian relative of the English word "shoot." Soon thereafter skeet fields began to spring up all around the country.

It didn't take long for people to catch on to the idea that there were records to be set and broken in this new game. The very year of the launching, H. M. Jackson, Jr., of Garner, North Carolina became the first man ever to break twenty-five targets straight. During the following year, the first national championship was won by the Raleigh Skeet Club of North Carolina. Also in 1926, the first skeet advertisement had appeared in the *Sportsman.* As evidence of faith in the new sport, the Remington Arms Company established an experimental field the following year that became the forerunner of Lordship, its current gun club. And Remington was soon manufacturing special skeet loads as well. That year the National Skeet Shooting Association began.

In the years that followed, skeet became an increasingly popular sport. Today there are skeet fields all over the world, for it is now an Olympic sport as well, along with trapshooting. Aside from fulfilling its original intention of helping shooters everywhere to improve their field shooting, skeet today is also an intensely competitive sport, as the new names and new records that appear on the record books each year testify. One of the all-time greats of this sport is the author of this book, D. Lee Braun. He is regarded with admiration and affection as about the greatest skeet instructor and competitor ever to walk down the line.

Lee Braun, a happy champion at Sun Valley in 1964, after winning overall tournament, the Shoshone Indian Shoot, which included trap and skeet.

D. LEE BRAUN: DAYS AT SKEET

■   There are circumstances surrounding the early years of my life that I have not been able to understand to this day. I was born on January 11, 1911, in Houston. Shortly thereafter we moved to the little country town of Milano Junction in Milam County, Texas, where I spent the first eleven years of my life. During this period my family and I lived with my grandparents, Mr. and Mrs. J. D. Peeples.

My grandfather and his two sons were avid hunters. Naturally, there grew in me that typical boyhood desire to have a gun of my own. At first I was continually and always trying to get me a BB gun, and then later a 22 and a shotgun. But despite the presence of hunters and guns in my grandfather's household, I was not allowed anything during these eleven years, not even the BB gun. This made no sense to me then, and it makes no sense to me now, either.

It seems to me that when any youngster wants to shoot, a parent should take him to a competent instructor to learn the use and safe handling of guns. And I would suggest that such begin-   **15** ners be given a few simple demonstrations of the wallop packed by various guns, including even a .22, to impress upon them the fact that they aren't dealing with toys any more. If a youngster wants to learn rifle shooting, *American Rifleman* magazine gives the locations of many rifle clubs where competent instructors can be found to teach the safe use of firearms. And most shotgun clubs will have two or three instructors available to help youngsters learn.

In my own case, though I was not allowed to have a gun as a youngster, my desire to shoot remained as strong as ever. And during a year in which I attended a military high school I learned how to use a rifle safely and correctly, under the proper direction. The result was that I made the rifle team that year. This was actually my start in competitive shooting, and it further increased my desire to continue my efforts in the shooting game. Finally, after graduating from Southern Methodist University in 1934, I went to work for the Remington Arms Company as a field representative, the youngest of the company's new employees at that time. During my first two years with Remington I had little opportunity to shoot. However, on July 4th of that first year, Colonel Joe Speight took me to the Dallas Gun Club and introduced me to skeet.

The First 25 Straight

I can remember that day as though it were yesterday. I was filled with all kinds of emotions—fear, anticipation, excitement, determination, and happiness. In that first round I broke 12 targets out of the 25 and felt as if I had just won a world championship or something. For the next two years, when I was able to find the time and the opportunity, I practiced at various gun clubs around Texas.

In those days, there were very few instructors. It was more or less a matter of digging it out for yourself. So I practiced all the systems and every way I could think of to improve myself as a shooter. It took me ten months before I had broken my first 25 straight, a memorable event in any shooter's life and one that also

16

seems to have happened no longer ago than yesterday.

It was drizzling rain at the Dallas Gun Club that morning. I was shooting an old double-barreled Parker hammer shotgun of my grandfather's, which had been given to me. I was making no real intense effort to achieve anything except to see what I could do with this old gun. Well, before I knew it I was at Station 7 and ready for my optional. At that moment the dawn broke, and I realized I had not missed a target up to that point. I became so nervous and excited it's a wonder I didn't miss the optional by a mile. Well, I didn't, and thus got my first 25. I ran off the field immediately, jumped into my car and drove home to tell the family what a great shot I had just become. It was like Thanksgiving Day and Christmas rolled into one.

Some time after this 25 straight, my old boss and old friend, Dewey Godfrey, sensing my desire and determination to become a good shooter, made it possible for me to attend various state, regional, and sectional shoots. In all of these I gained more and more experience in divesting myself of the unnecessary thoughts and movements that would reduce my ability to shoot well.

Several other people were going for me in this period, too. One was Felix S. ''Red'' Hawkins of Dallas, who at the time held the high overall record for broken targets of 544 x 550, a record I would one day have the honor of breaking. Another was Roy Cherry, also of Dallas. These two fellows guyed me and goaded me mercilessly, teaching me the hard way about performing under pressure.

Important to me also was Grant Ilseng of Houston, who impressed on my mind over and over again the importance of concentrating only on the very next target, not worrying about befores and afters or anything else that might be going on. I will go into the importance of this later, when we come to the principles of shooting. It is paramount. As far as I know, Grant was the first man to emphasize how really important that idea is.

Working and learning with people of this caliber, coupled with my own burning desire to perfect my game, brought me to my peak of proficiency with the 12-gauge gun in 1941. It was in **17**

With aerial gunnery shotguns, a championship Laredo team kneels before Lieut. Mike Zerance, Capt. Lee Braun, Maj. Buddy Jones, Ed Palma.

that year that I shot the highest average recorded up to that time, a .996, breaking 1021 targets out of 1025. This record stood until Ed Scherer broke it in 1957 with a .9975.

A Major Contribution

Just as I hit my stride, World War II came along and folded up the skeet game, as it did so many other things. I entered the army with a first lieutenant's commission in the infantry, but was transferred to the air corps. I soon became a gunnery instructor, as did many other good shooters of the time. In 1942 I was put in charge of the flexible gunnery range at the air force's central school in Laredo, Texas. Our basic job was to train student gunners to use the flexible machine guns in B-24 and B-17 bombers. On trap and skeet fields we employed shotguns to teach new gunners how to lead targets the way they would have to lead passing enemy airplanes. To help them get the feel of the actual guns, we also used machine-gun mounts with shotguns installed on them. Training progressed from there to the use of actual 30- and 50-caliber machine guns fired at sleeve targets towed by airplanes.

18

For awhile it looked as though the war had killed off clay target shooting around the country, but actually this was not the case. Some of the finest shots in our present-day shooting game came from those wartime training camps.

I had never shot very much trap until trapshooting was instituted in our training program at Laredo. There the fine points of the sport were given me by Mercer Tenille and Cliff Doughman, two very close friends. I was able to reciprocate with Cliff by teaching him to shoot skeet, at which he became very proficient indeed.

So skeet did survive the war, as I did. I was discharged from the army early in 1945 with the rank of major. Since I had accumulated considerable leave of absence, I did not return to work at Remington until the following year. During this interval I was able to attend the national skeet championships in Indianapolis as an amateur, because I had been in the armed forces for forty-four months and had not gone actively back to work for an arms manufacturer. There I won the 20-gauge championship with 100 straight, as well as the 28-gauge event with a 96.

High Overall—a New Record

Shortly thereafter came another satisfying accomplishment, which equaled the thrill of my first 25 straight. It happened in Syracuse, New York, at the National Skeet Shoot in 1947, after I had returned to Remington. My old friend Felix Hawkins of Dallas had previously set a high overall record in 1940 with 544 x 550. In the overall event you shoot 100 targets with the 410-gauge gun, 100 with the 28-gauge, the same with a 20-gauge, and 250 targets with a 12-gauge, making a total of 550 targets with the four guns. That is what makes this an overall event—it requires that you be a top shot with all four guns used in skeet.

At the 1947 National I was able to break Red Hawkins' old record of 544 x 550 with a 546. This in itself was quite a thrill. But *how* I broke this record was one of the highlights of my shooting career. In the 410-gauge event I had misssed four targets in the first two rounds of 25 shots each, High 4 on the second field being the last target I dropped. In the third and fourth rounds I broke 50 straight, giving me a 67 straight in the 410-gauge event. Thereafter I broke 100 straight with the 28, 100 straight with the 20, and 250 straight with the 12, for the record 546 x 550. In addition, the long run of 517 targets with four guns, after missing four targets in the first two rounds with the 410-gauge but not missing one thereafter, is a record that has yet to be broken.

However, that high overall record was tied three times. And finally, as ultimately happens to all records, it was broken in 1964 by Bill Sesnon, III of Los Angeles. Bill racked up an incredible 548 x 550, including 100 straight down the line with the 410. I take considerable pride in the fact that it was Bill who broke this record, because I had started working with him from scratch just a few years back.

Believe It or Not

In the course of setting the high overall record at Syracuse, I had also won the 12-gauge skeet championship with 250 x 250. That same year I went on to Vandalia, Ohio, for the Grand American Trap Shoot. There I encountered two of the greatest moments of pressure of my shooting career. The first came when I found myself shooting off with Cap Greer, an old hand and a wonderful trap shot, for the North American Clay Target Championship. The shoot-off lasted one round, in which Cap dropped a target and I was fortunate enough to continue and break the round straight. However, I was so nervous that it was almost impossible to keep myself under control, for this was my first shoot-off as a pro at the Grand. Cap was a formidable opponent and my desire to win this event had me so keyed up that I was very lucky to get by.

To my knowledge, this is the only time anyone has won both the 12-gauge skeet championship with a 250 x 250 and the North American Clay Target Championship for trapshooting with a 200 x 200 during the same year. Because of this, I shortly thereafter found myself in Ripley's "Believe It or Not" column. My wife's reaction to this was that it only verified what she had been saying all along—I was a character, and now she had proof.

Top: Record-breaking Squad 11—Smith, Feltus, Morris, Doughman and Braun. Bottom left: Grant Ilseng. Bottom right: Braun and Jack Eliot.

The second big moment of pressure during the 1947 Grand American occurred while I was shooting as a member of a five-man squad which included Ralph Smith, Morell Feltus, Cecil Morris and Cliff Doughman. We had gone down the line in the morning and there had been only three targets dropped by the entire squad during the first 100-target event, in which each man shoots 100 targets.

On the Firing Line

During the afternoon, as we proceeded with our shooting, I became conscious of a lot of murmuring in the background. At first I didn't pay much attention to it. But on our last round the noise became so noticeable that I turned around and looked. There must have been five or six thousand people watching us.

Naturally I began wondering what the big attraction was, when it came to me all at once that only one target had been missed by our entire squad that afternoon. Here we were, with the opportunity to tie the world record five-man squad score, which was 499 x 500 at that time. All of this I had in mind when suddenly it was my shot, the last shot of the round. And I knew I had to hit this next target to tie that record.

I had my gun to my shoulder and was about to call for the target when I realized I was totally unprepared, mentally or physically, to shoot that target. My mind was on what we might be able to accomplish, instead of the target that was about to sail out there.

I took my gun down from my shoulder and stood there looking out over the shooting field. If I missed this target, there would be nowhere to go hide except the trap house. I couldn't disappear, or anything else, and it depended entirely upon me whether or not we tied this score. Well, I got myself ready, mentally and physically, called for the target—and fortunately, I broke it. So we tied the world record. In the course of this, with the 497 x 500 that we had shot in the morning, we set a new squad record of 996 x 1000, which still stands today. I will never forget the immense pressure under which I shot that last target. For if I had missed I don't know what in the world I would have done, except probably faint.

It's hard work to win any kind of championship or set any kind of record. Consequently, I am proud of the many national championships I have won. Jimmy Robinson, skeet and trap editor for *Sports Afield* magazine, has honored me by placing me on eighteen of his All-American skeet teams and fourteen All-American trap teams. I am certainly proud of that, too.

It feels good to break and set records—but it doesn't pay to let winning become an obsession. The first time you win a national tournament or set a world record, buy a cup of coffee and tell them at the counter what you have just done. Then see how much they take off the price of the coffee. What counts is the compensation you get personally for achieving something you wanted to achieve.

I would suggest to any young shooter just beginning in this game that if he can listen to some old hands who are real champions, and pick up some of their pointers, he can eliminate a lot of time and trial and error. With this in mind I would like to offer some observations, and also a few incidents in the shooting game that I will always remember because they taught me so much.

Team Shooting

You will often hear people say that a shooter cannot shoot both skeet and trap. But this just isn't so. Many shooters have done wonderfully well at both, for instance Grant Ilseng, Joe Devers, Rudy Etchen, Cliff Doughman and Fred Missildine. I could name a host of others. And I have proved this point to myself to my own satisfaction.

The real difficulty here is the time problem. Ordinarily a shooter doesn't really have the time to participate in both games to the fullest and be in his best form for each. A fellow would nearly have to be twins to accomplish this. But don't let this difficulty deter you from shooting either one or the other on occasion, for the shooting principles are exactly the same. The only change is that the targets are thrown from different positions and travel in different directions.

23

As a shooter progresses and breaks better and better scores, he will have the opportunity of shooting on a team of some sort. Replacements are continually in demand, especially on a five-man team, and shooters are always looking for a two-man team partnership when they go to local shoots or championships. But be forewarned: Team shooting is tough on a shooter, particularly a new shooter. For he will tend to worry not only about his own performance but about how well he compares to the other members of the team. He will feel they are watching him, and perhaps secretly criticizing him, which can make for some very intense pressure on the new team member.

Relax!

An old-timer once gave me one of the most important tips I ever got. It concerned the simple matter of relaxation. His advice was this: If you are in a long run or a championship, or have another straight to shoot or a shoot-off coming up tomorrow, have a moderately early dinner, about 7 o'clock or 7:30; then either go to a picture show, or bowl, or something of the sort, until 10 or 11 o'clock; after that, go to bed. By then the mind will be relieved of thinking of the coming day, how many targets you want to shoot or whom you'll have to shoot against. You can then get a pretty sound sleep and get up mentally and physically ready for the next day.

But if you try to overtrain and go to bed early, all you'll do is lie there and shoot targets all night. You'll be a mental wreck the next day as well as a physical wreck. And the shoot-off or tournament or whatever it is will have gone by the board before your first shot is fired.

A real sportsman will tell you this sort of thing, but there are some shooters who won't. For there are pitfalls for a shooter as he begins to win championships. When a fellow is new and just starting, everybody pats him on the back and gives him a lot of encouragement. But when he begins to steal the thunder and the championships, it's another story—from a minority of shooters anyway. They become resentful. At this point you will discover that in this game, as in any other, not every man is a sportsman.

Nice Guys Finish First

I was in a national tournament in the 410-gauge event and was on Station 4, which is a hard station with any gun. This competitor came up and stopped me, just as I was about to call for my target, and asked what the number of my squad was. He knew perfectly well what it was. If he didn't, all he had to do was to look at the scorekeeper's pad. He was trying to get my concentration off the business at hand, with the hope that I might drop a target or two. I realized immediately what he was up to. But instead of making me wrap the gun around his head, as I was inclined to do, this ploy just increased my determination. I went on and won the championship. Later I dropped by and thanked him for giving me this double impetus to concentrate on what I was doing.

Another story of poor sportsmanship that backfired concerns a friend of mine. It was in the shoot-off of a national tournament, where my friend was shooting in the number-one spot in the shoot-off. After he had shot Low 1 he walked over and was standing behind Station 2, a good distance away from the shooter following him. His competitor at Station 1 called the referee and said, "Would you please have that man move from the position he is in? He is bothering me. I can see him out of the corner of my eye."

My friend moved back as the referee suggested. After shooting Station 2, he not only got out of sight but melted into the crowd that was watching the shoot-off. The competitor, on finishing his shots at Station 2, turned around and could not see my friend anywhere. In somewhat of a confused state he asked, "Where *is* he?" My friend emerged from the crowd and asked, "Is it all right now for me to go up to Station 3 and shoot my targets?" This so disconcerted the other man that before the round was over he had dropped three targets. This is usually the end result of such shenanigans.

Don't let yourself lose your temper or blame something or somebody for missing a target. *You* were the one who had the gun **25**

Top: Mike and Mark Pelkey with their parents; Ed Scherer. Center: Vermillion, Hilburn. Bottom: Rogers, Braun, Jr., Horner, Allen, Laird.

in your hands. *You* were the one who pointed the barrel and pulled the trigger. And if the target was missed, it was *you* who missed it. If you felt you weren't in control of yourself, you should have taken the gun down and started over again.

Remember, when you walk up to that station to shoot your target, you haven't got a friend in the world. Everyone else there is trying to do exactly the same thing you are—to break every target. So when you go up to shoot, eliminate everything from your mind except the factors that must be present to break *the next target.*

Shooting for the Moon

Another thing to remember—and this is even more important —is that sometimes you can outsmart yourself. I'll never forget one occasion on which I did this. I was in a registered shoot at Lordship, Connecticut, the Remington Gun Club. This club, under the best conditions, is the sportiest skeet course I know of in this country. It is out on a peninsula and usually breezy, which makes for erratic targets. Moreover, the fields are set at various angles, so that as you move from one to another the wind conditions change. On this day I had broken 99 with the 410-gauge and only the optional target remained for 100 straight with this gun in a registered tournament—a very rare occurrence. With only the optional left, the incoming target at Station 7 and the easiest shot on the skeet field, I had completely relaxed and accustomed myself to the idea that it was in the bag. There was nothing to it now. As far as I was concerned it was all over except the shooting and the scoring.

I called for the target, calmly and deliberately raised my gun, got the proper lead, pulled the trigger—and forgot to follow through. I watched dumbfounded as that target sailed by like a great big moon. Imagine my consternation, my disconcertion, my sickness of stomach, heart and mind! The gamut of feelings, emotions and thoughts that ran through me is indescribable. Even today I can recall the color of the sky, the pale blue haze, and the exact way that target looked as it floated by without a nick in it. **27**

For a time I held the long run 410-gauge record of 153 straight targets. But I never did break 100 down the line with the 410. That day at Lordship was the closest I ever came, and I've never forgotten the lesson taught me: Don't count your score *until it's on the scoreboard.*

These are examples of how you can goof yourself up on the skeet field, and of how there are always some individuals around who will try to help you do this if you don't have the misfortune and lapse of mind to do it for yourself. But most of my memories of the skeet field are fond ones—of good shooting, good sportsmanship and many good friends.

The Lady is a Winner

One incident I'll never forget involved the sportsmanship of Grant Ilseng, a man I think exemplifies that word in its highest meaning. The occasion was a handicap event at a large shoot several years back, in which each shooter was allowed to drop a certain number of targets, determined by his shooting average. In this event there was a young lady from Dallas, who had a 12-target handicap. She could drop 12 targets out of 100 before the referee considered she had missed one. Grant Ilseng, being a Class AA shooter, had no handicap and so could not miss any targets. There was a third shooter in this shoot-off who had been handicapped several targets, perhaps several too many. At least Grant felt there was no justification for the number of targets the man had been handicapped.

So the shoot-off began. It went 20 rounds, 500 targets for each shooter. Grant Ilseng broke his 500 targets one by one down to this 20th round, when the other man in the shoot-off finally dropped one too many. That left only Grant and the young lady, going into the 21st round. It was at this point in the shoot-off that Grant missed a target.

I happened to be sitting right behind him when he pulled the trigger. And a man of his prowess just doesn't miss a target by 10 feet, which is how far he missed that one, because I saw the streak of the shot as it passed behind the target. The young lady had tried so hard to do the very best she could in this long shoot-off in spite of the hardships, that Grant in turn was doing his very best to see that she was not outshot by what he considered incorrect and unfair handicapping.

After the shoot-off had gone to a very happy lady, he and I were walking over to get a cold drink at the refreshment stand and I asked him, in a leading kind of a way, "How far did you miss that target, one or two feet?" He just chuckled and said, "Aw, shut up," and we went on.

There are not many shooters who would give up any kind of championship if they had the opportunity to win it. But here was a man who tried to protect this young girl for 500 shots, and then was happy to let her win. Grant had already won many national championships. One more win meant nothing to him compared to the sportsmanship that he felt was called for on this particular afternoon.

Superstitious Shooters

After a new shooter has won his first few tournaments there's a very good chance that he'll find himself developing that psychological quirk known as superstition. Having won in a certain kind of hat or cap or some other kind of shooting apparel, he sometimes develops a kind of fixation on these garments. And any suggestion of giving them up would be like telling the fellow to kick a rattlesnake in the face—barefooted. Shooters are notoriously a superstitious lot.

I certainly am no exception. For years I used the same old cap and jacket, even though the bill of the cap was frayed and the shoulder pad of my shooting coat was wearing out. I had shot well in them and the thought of going into a tournament without this cap and coat was, to me, like going into a lion's den without a gun. I suppose I would still be wearing them if my wife hadn't taken it on herself to throw them in the garbage can without my knowledge. The atmosphere around our house was pretty unpleasant after I discovered she had disposed of my shooting garments. Eventually, however, I found out that it isn't the clothes that 29 make the shooter, and things returned to normal. I must say, though, that I'm still superstitious about many things in this game.

Usually such quirks are relatively harmless. Sometimes, however, being superstitious can pull the string on you, as it did on my good friend Jack Boardman at the National Skeet Shoot in Dallas in 1951. Jack is a tremendous shot, and at this time had shot over 1,000 targets straight with the 12-gauge gun. Everyone at the tournament, of course, was aware of this fact. Well, Jack approached me at the Remington exhibit tent and said, "Pappy, I wish you would come over to the practice field and watch me on Station 1." I looked at him, wondering what he was talking about. He couldn't be serious. Just the same, I said, "Okay, boy, come on and I'll try to teach you what to do." When we got to the field, he stood at Station 1 and shot High 1 six or eight times, asking me all the while if I saw anything wrong. Since he was powdering these targets one after another, I couldn't figure out what he was getting at. I knew he was under a bit of tension and wanted to run his string as far as possible in the 12-gauge event the following day. Still, as I watched him, I could see that there was nothing the slightest bit wrong with the way he was breaking those targets. So I remained puzzled.

As the 12-gauge event started the next day, his dad, Clayton Boardman, came to see me and said, "Well, Jack just did it. He missed the first target out." I just couldn't believe it. High 1 is a hard target to miss. But then his dad went on: "I could kill this fellow who phoned him last night—or, rather, the night we got here." The man, it turned out, had called Jack Boardman and said: "I had a dream, Jack, that you were going to miss your first target out." This, of course, began to prey on his superstitious mind. And this was why he had been worrying me about watching him shoot High 1. The fellow's dream had become a fixation in Jack's mind, so he actually missed the first target out, after having broken over 1,000 straight.

Making the rounds of various shoots naturally makes it possible to witness some spectacular events. I take a father's pride in

Prized teacher. Mercer Tenille (with wife Vivian). On right: Raymond Smith, Braun, Elaine Hoag, Annan and Jay Schatz, skeet supporters.

recalling one that involved my son, Joe Lee Braun, and his boyhood friend Jack Horner, who was practically a member of the family. I taught both these kids to shoot from scratch. In 1953, when they were in their early teens, they went to the National Skeet Shoot in Reno. Shooting as a two-man team as they frequently did, these youngsters wound up contending for the 28-gauge championship against two old AA shooters, Herman Ehler and another old-timer. The wind was blowing very hard and the targets were erratic, but the two boys had nothing in the world on their minds but breaking every target. And they were doing quite well at it.

It became quite obvious that the shooting pressure was buildup in Herman and his partner. Here were two upstart kids shooting off in a championship event against them and holding their own very well. You could see the tension in the two men's faces, and they dropped a target here and there. But the boys each broke 25 straight. When it was all over they had won the national two-man team 28-gauge championship. And don't think I wasn't tickled pink.

Another memorable bit of shooting involved Arnold Reiger, **31** one of the great trapshooters. It began at the Grand American Trapshooting Tournament in Vandalia, Ohio. I was shooting on a five-man squad with Arnold, and at the end of the first 100 targets we had both missed two. As we walked off the field Arnold came over and said, ''I wish I could have broken that 100 straight. It would have helped my confidence.'' As it turned out, the two targets he dropped while shooting that first 100 were the last he missed all week long in the program and in the various shoot-offs he participated in.

At this particular Grand, Arnold was shooting Peters shells. And being with Remington-Peters I was of course particularly interested in his success. Consequently, as the week wore on and his string got longer and longer, I grew more and more nervous, hoping he would break the existing record, which had been shot with competitive ammunition. In the course of the week the little guy almost caused me heart failure a hundred times. He shot broken targets, outlaw targets, fast pulls and slow pulls and two targets which he didn't even call for. He just shot everything that came out of the trap house. And he never came near missing one. With all this on my mind, the scores I myself shot at the Grand that particular year would make you think I had never held a shotgun in my hands.

For the benefit of readers who are not that familiar with trap rules, a broken target is one that flies out of the house in fragments, broken by the trap mechanism before the shooter gets a chance to shoot at it. If he then shoots at the fragments and misses, he buys it and the result is scored. An outlaw target is one that comes at too wide an angle out of the trap. A slow pull comes a second or so after the shooter calls for the target. A fast pull comes before the shooter calls for it.

After the last target had been shot in the week's program and Arnold had 1007 straight, he grabbed my sleeve and asked, ''Lee, isn't the old record 1179?'' I said that it was. Then he made a remark to me indicating how little confidence he had that he could break this record. ''Well,'' said Arnold, ''let's go down to the practice trap and I'll break it.'' Practice targets don't count. Had we done that, it would merely have decreased his chances of continuing the streak, but that's how convinced Arnold was he could really break that record.

As it turned out, Arnold left the Grand when it was over and went to Salt Lake City, where he broke 300 straight targets in a registered shoot. From there he moved on to California and broke another 100 straight. His long run ended, finally, at 1434 targets, a rare phenomenon indeed in the trapshooting world.

Cream of the Crop

In the course of my life in skeet, I have naturally been asked many times who I think is or was the greatest shot in the world. Of course this is difficult, if not impossible, to answer because conditions and circumstances have changed over the years. Also, each shooter has his own idea of what he thinks makes a really great shot. A man can be an absolute wizard in some areas of shooting but not so good in others. So it depends on what you feel a great shooter should be when it comes to judging one or another of them. My idea of a great shooter is someone who is an all-around great shot, and I don't mean just the 12-gauge shotgun. I mean all the gauges and I mean shooting skeet, trap and live birds. I have to suggest this as my definition and my way of looking at the question of who is the greatest shot.

If I look at the question this way, there is no one I would choose above Grant Ilseng. I think he had no peer with all four gauges—12, 20, 28 and 410—in skeet and the other areas of shotgun shooting. However, other shooters have done tremendously well in the three classifications, too, and one of them is Rudy Etchen. Cliff Doughman also comes to mind. I think these would be about the toughest to compete with as all-around shotgun shooters in the three categories.

If we stick to skeet alone, which is our primary concern, I would feel as I do about shooting generally. I personally can't agree that the winner of the 12-gauge championship is the champion of any skeet shoot. I feel very strongly that the high overall shooter, the person who shoots all four gauges and brings in the highest score of anyone in a championship, is the winner and should be declared such.

With this in mind, I would say William Hay Rogers of Atherton, California, is one of the finest skeet shooters to emerge since 1951. In 1960 he had a .9847 average with all four guns for a record high overall. The following year he upped his average to .9855, an overall amateur record that stands to date. And while on the subject of great overall skeet shooters, the name of Alex Kerr of Beverly Hills, California, comes immediately to mind.

Long runs are not to be overlooked, either. And here one has to recognize the tremendous concentration and stamina of Pete Candy of Encino, California, who, through the years 1961 to 1963, established a record long run at skeet of 1589 straight. This was one of the greatest feats in 12-gauge shotgun-shooting history.

We cannot discuss great shooters and leave out the women. Don't believe that just because a shooter is a woman she isn't capable of pointing a gun and shooting just as good a score as a man. As I write this, the lady that comes immediately to mind is Carola Mandel of Chicago. In 1956 she shot the highest 12-gauge shotgun average with a .994. That was of *all* shooters for that year, men *and* women, making it a really outstanding feat.

With Carola, I have to mention such greats as Ann Martin Hecker, Janice Jenkens Mason, Judy Allen, Betje Annan, Daphne Muchnic, Jo Ann Wallis, Otelia Deckshot, Kathleen McGinn Sedlecky, Diane Coulter and Clarine Menzel. Clarine won the women's title at the National Skeet Shoot in 1966 and also beat out many of the men in the 20-gauge event with 100 x 100. So don't underestimate the women. There are a number around, and more and more are coming up, who are capable of giving the best men shooters in the country a run for the big prizes, and of carting them home to boot!

When I think of up-and-coming young people I immediately think of a pleasure I have had over the last fifteen years that, for me, ranks with shooting itself. This is the teaching of youngsters, both boys and girls, to become successful shots. Watching them learn and progress is a real joy. They are very intense, and every-

Typical Braun squad at a National shoot in Rochester, N. Y. From left: Mike Annan, Daphne Muchnic, Elsa Young, Braun and Bill Coberly.

thing is so important to them. You have to handle them carefully to get the most out of them. You have to be harsh with them at times to make them understand the realities not only of the shooting game but life itself. Learning to shoot has many implications for youngsters. It teaches them to rely on themselves and gives them self-confidence and character. It teaches them safety, consideration of others, being good sports, and the facts about competition—which all too soon they will find themselves up against in the actualities of life. And it gives them a great deal of pleasure in this world that they would otherwise miss.

I have had many parents ask me at what age they should let kids learn to shoot. The proper age is when they can handle a gun and not let the gun handle them. This calls to mind a young friend of mine, Mark Pelkey, who started shooting at the age of nine. His dad asked me to personally see that his guns were fitted to him properly, which I did. This young fellow, at the age of ten, shot over 5000 registered skeet targets. At present he is shooting excellent scores. I imagine you'll hear from him soon.

Among the girls, I am equally proud of Diane Vermillion of Sherman Oaks, California. I was fortunate in witnessing a tre-

Women champions Braun helped: Carola Mandel and Anne Martin Hecker, Clarine Menzel and Diane Coulter, Betje Annan with Bill Brown.

mendous performance of hers at the National Skeet Shoot in Reno in 1964. There, at the age of thirteen, this young lady broke the following scores as a sub-junior: 95 out of 100 in the 410-gauge, 97 x 100 in the 28-gauge, 96 x 100 with the 20 and 237 x 250 with the 12—for a high overall score of 525 out of 550. Such shooting by a 13-year-old in national competition is not only an outstanding feat, but shows that desire and determination, concentration and know-how, whatever the age or sex, are all that it takes for a fine performance.

Looking back over the years, I can recall many such youngsters it was a real pleasure to work with—Barney Hilburn of Dallas, my first youngster to achieve national prominence; Jo Ann Wallis of Piedmont, California, my first Junior girl star; and many more, some of whose pictures appear here. I treasure each of them.

I have taught my share of adults too, (with one exception that I will come to later), and they present a different problem. It is much easier to take brand-new shooters, young boys or girls, and teach them to shoot. Their minds are open and they will accept your instruction and work on it as it is given them. But shooters who are already well along in the game and have formed bad habits are a real problem. They must begin by undoing these old habits and learning new ones.

This always results in a shooter's score dropping considerably below where it had been. That's hard on the ego of most shooters. They cannot accept the fact that for a while they won't be shooting the 24s and 25s they are accustomed to shoot. They begin to grumble when they find themselves shooting 18s, 19s and 20s. They also lose faith that ultimately they will be shooting more 25s than anything else. However, those who are willing to accept this setback will eventually recoup and perfect their shooting. Those who are not willing to accept it will go along and continue to break their 25s, 23s, 22s and 24s, and of course that will never get them to the top in this game.

One particularly difficult person to instruct is the successful businessman. He feels that he has been a success in his personal **37** endeavor, and it is hard for him to understand why he cannot just take up a shotgun and have the same degree of success in shooting —and do it in a hurry. But clay targets are no respecters of persons, whatever their positions may be in the world.

My Worst Student

Despite the difficulties presented by some pupils, I never had but one that I gave up on. This was my dad, God bless and rest his soul. It happened around 1949, when I was visiting my folks on Labor Day. The dove season was opening that day, and I wanted to give Dad some of the pleasure that I had had at shooting. He had worked hard all his life from about the age of twelve, and had very little of the kind of pleasure I had in shooting. I asked him if he would like to go dove hunting with me. He said he'd be glad to go, but he didn't know very much about shooting. Actually, he had never shot a gun before that time. He was then about fifty-eight or fifty-nine.

I took him to an old tank, a dammed-up area for holding water in dry weather, about six or seven miles out of Milano. You could get wonderful wing shooting there on doves flying in from the feeding fields to water. I gave him one of my Remington pump shotguns and showed him how to load and use it safely. Then we settled down and waited for the doves to fly in. Knowing he was new at shooting, I stood a little behind him.

When the first bunch came in, Dad got so excited he was trying to hit all the birds with one shot. He was waving that gun as though it was a flag on the Fourth of July. I stood by him for several shots, but couldn't get through to him. He was so excited trying to hit the birds that he didn't pay the slightest attention to me.

The tank had high banks and finally, seeing that I was making no impression whatever, I moved around to the opposite side of the bank and started shooting my birds. Every time I hit one he'd holler, "I got him! I got him!" I doubt that he came within twelve or fourteen feet of any bird he shot at.

But we had fun, and we got home safely. And believe you me,

At a Reno National, promoted by Ray Smith, Lee poses with his students Jo Ann Wallis, Thelma Anguish, John Di Gardi, Henry duPont, III.

I was never so glad to get home. I never let my dad know he had scared me half to death.

I would like to close this sketch of my life with the story of the greatest compliment I ever received while helping others improve their shooting. The story concerns Lathrop Brown, a gentleman, a friend, and one of the finest sportsmen I have ever known in my years of shooting.

The story begins at the National Skeet Shoot in Las Vegas in 1948. Lathrop Brown approached me one day at the Remington exhibit tent, introduced himself, and said he would like to discuss with me the philosophy of skeet and its relation to everyday life. I had not met him before, and therefore did not know who he was. It happened that there was no opportunity for us to get together, because this was a rather hectic shoot with a very big attendance, many shoot-offs to arrange, and so on down the line. So the proposed visit never came about.

Some months later, however, I was at my home in Dallas one **39**

Sunday night when the phone rang. The conversation began with: "Professor, I have come to sit at your feet for a week." The operator had told me the call was coming from Mineral Wells, Texas, and I searched my mind trying to figure out who was calling and who would start off a conversation this way. After talking for some time, I finally identified the man on the other end as this same Lathrop Brown. I agreed to meet him at the Baker Hotel in Dallas the next day.

He and his wife Helen had come all the way from San Francisco. I was still curious about this visit. As our talk progressed he again remarked, "Professor, I have driven over 2,100 miles for you to teach me how to shoot." This was puzzling, because I knew that the gentleman already knew how to shoot. Naturally, I wondered just what he was driving at. There was nothing to do but ask him bluntly what he meant, particularly considering the fact that he was getting on in years at this time, which should make adapting to something new particularly difficult.

Well, he said he had been using the swing-through method of shooting and could not seem to attain the scores he felt he was capable of shooting. The idea of changing a style of shooting he had been using his entire life worried me no end. I had to say that although I would be more than happy to give him all the assistance I could, I wondered if he had taken into consideration the possibility that imposing my basic instruction onto the way he was shooting might confuse him to the point where he would no longer be able to shoot as well as he was shooting now.

With no hesitation he said: "Professor, you teach me the way you shoot and let's see what happens." This was on a Monday, and I arranged to meet him at the Dallas Gun Club that afternoon. Every afternoon that week I worked with him from one o'clock until dark. During the mornings he would practice the things we had discussed the afternoon before. Through all those long hours his good wife Helen sat patiently in the car and waited. So the week went.

On the next Sunday morning he said, "Professor, I think we should have a graduation exercise today."

"In what respect do you mean that, Mr. Brown?" I was quick to ask.

"We must have a tournament," he told me.

"Well, that would be fine," I responded.

"What would you like to shoot, and how many targets?"

He proposed that we shoot 50 with the 410, 50 with the 28, and 100 each with the 20- and 12-gauge guns. Then he added, "Now that we have set the program, I think we should have a wager." As I started to suggest that this wasn't really necessary, he cut in: "Professor, if you really believe in your way of shooting, then you can't possibly back down from any sort of wager that I might propose."

Seeming to have no alternative, I said: "All right, sir, you name the game and I'll try to play it." Whereupon he asked if I thought shooting for the shells and targets would be an appropriate wager. I thought that would be fine, so we got our shells and our guns and started out to the skeet field for the graduation exercise.

The result was that I broke 50 straight with the 410 and Mr. Brown broke 48. The score was identical with the 28. With the 20-gauge, I broke 100 straight and he broke 98. And in the 12-gauge event, we tied at 99. I still cannot comprehend this. He had completely changed the method of shooting he had been using all his life. Yet in one short week of following instructions and eliminating old methods, Lathrop Brown had progressed to this astonishing degree of proficiency.

Lathrop and Helen Brown became two of the warmest friends I have ever had, and it is almost in reverence that I tell this story. For a more gracious gentleman I never met. As I learned later, he returned to California and broke 200 straight in a 12-gauge tournament. And he went on to win many championships after that, and was still shooting in tournaments when he was in his 70s. He has passed on now. But he lives with me wherever I go, wherever there are shooters and wherever there are tournaments, as a living comparison with those you sometimes hear say: "I can't do this," and so forth and so on.

PRINCIPLES
OF SKEET

Demonstrating pointing, the author extends forefinger under fore-end to guide and point the gun as though it were an extension of the finger.

■ There are a number of principles in shooting skeet that a shooter must work on and try to master if he is to improve and perfect his shooting, and thereby derive the real pleasure to be had in doing well at this sport. But for the most part, these principles are not unique to skeet. They will improve your field shooting just as much. And we must keep in mind that the improvement of field shooting was the reason behind the invention of skeet to start with. There is nothing esoteric or mystical about these principles. They are simply the fundamentals of good shotgun shooting, whatever the flying target is at which you're shooting.

As I have noted earlier, back in the days when there were few good instructors, I experimented with various systems to see what elements they had to offer that would improve my own shooting. Some ideas seemed to work for me and some didn't. Considering all these, I tried to get at what seemed to me were the real essentials required for each shot, eliminating all unnecessary movements and thoughts. The result was my own system of shooting. I do not say it is *the* system, nor that I invented the elements of it—since many were gathered from other methods of shooting, as I have said. I do maintain, though, that following my study and my trial and error period, my shooting reached its peak, and that my method worked consistently afterwards. It has also worked well for many a fine shooter who has come to me for advice.

The principles of shooting are three—mechanical, physical, and psychological. By far the most important of all of them is a psychological principle—control and concentration as you shoot each target. This is also the most difficult principle to master. But unless it *is* mastered, all the other fundamentals in the world will not help much. Control is the prime principle that makes the others work for you. For this reason, its significance will be most clear after we have gone over the other fundamentals. So, let's begin with the mechanical ones.

Gun Fit

One most important factor at the very beginning is that your gun should fit you personally and individually. Most gun manufacturers make their guns to specifications that will fit the majority of shooters. At least, I know Remington does. Ladies' guns must have a bit more down-pitch in the stock, because certain differences in female physical structure require this. Moreover some men, with physiques somewhat different from the average, may require a longer stock, shorter stock, or some other such adjustment. This can easily be done by a good gunsmith or stock maker.

This raises the question of how to tell if a gun does fit you. A very simple test will give you the answer. Close your eyes, then raise the gun to your face and shoulder as though you were aiming it. Now open your eyes. The bead on the end of the barrel should be seen resting right in the groove on the top of the receiver, or right on top of the ventilated rib if it is other than a plain-barrel shotgun. It should not be above it, so that you see a stretch of the barrel in between. Nor should it be below the groove, so the bead is obscured.

In making this test, one important point has to be made concerning how to raise a gun. Most people make the mistake of raising a gun to the shoulder and then lowering their heads, pressing the cheek to the stock to sight along the gun barrel. This is absolutely incorrect, because it produces a tenseness in the neck muscles—and any tenseness in the body when shooting will reduce your ability to break targets. You have to be completely relaxed to shoot effectively. So raise the gun to your face and shoulder. Don't lay your face down to the stock.

I am a real nut when it comes to guns and their fit. When you find a gun that fits you and you can shoot well with it, never let anyone talk you into disposing of it or trading it for any reason whatever. I find many people who are unwilling to accept the fact that *they* might miss a target. The blame always belongs somewhere else, and usually on the gun—even though the week before they shot a 200 straight with it. These people are continually trading and trying new guns and, of course, every time they do so, the weight and balance and pointability changes. As a result, they're always adjusting to new guns and always missing targets.

As the reader is aware by now, four guns are used in shooting skeet—the 410, 28, 20 and 12. So if you intend to shoot this game you will need these four guns. It is important that these guns have identical specifications as to stock length, drop, pitch and balance, so that you will have the same feeling no matter which gauge you are shooting. I have used both a pump and an automatic shotgun at skeet. And before Remington discontinued the Model 32 over-and-under, I used that gun. Currently I am using four Remington automatics. These guns have interchangeable parts with other Remington guns, which can become important at times. For instance, if you are shooting a tournament in one of the gauges and break a firing pin, you can easily pirate the item from a similar model. This is a lot better than borrowing a gun, because you are still using your own equipment and don't have a new gun and a new feel to contend with.

Once you've got the gun or guns that fit you, there's another very important fundamental to face. This is safety—making sure no injury happens to you or (and I think this is much more important) to someone else. I think the highway slogan is wrong that reads: "Drive carefully. The life you save may be your own." I think this sign should read: "Drive carefully. The life you save may belong to someone else." And the same goes for shooting. Walk carefully, because you're carrying a big stick. Always walk or stand with a gun pointed toward the ground. When hunting, never load the gun until you are actually out in the field and are ready to hunt. And on the skeet field, never load your gun until you are at your station and are getting ready for your target.

The Grip

Now that you're at your station and ready to shoot, so to speak, we come to the question of how to grip the gun. Most new shotgun shooters regard a gun as a kind of cannon. When they fire they hang onto it for dear life, anticipating the heavy "kick". As with so many other things, the exact opposite is the right way.

Instead of grasping the fore-end, you should let it lie in your hand as though you were holding four or five eggs. Similarly, don't grip the stock and press it to your shoulder. Hold the gun **45** at all points in a relaxed manner, as though there would be no recoil at all. If you make a test and fire it this way, and then compare the feel to another shot when you grasp the gun tightly, you will feel the difference immediately. More important than comfort, however, is the fact that if you "muscle" the gun, you won't be able to track your flying target smoothly. Both in skeet and in the field, each of your shots must be a smooth, relaxed shot.

To get the correct feel, hold the gun loosely and extend your forefinger forward under the fore-end and in line with the barrel. Imagine the barrel as just an extension of this forefinger. In this relaxed way, imagine that you are simply moving your finger to point at a moving target or bird, just pointing and tracking it. Now if you let the gun go along with your hand that way, it will be much easier to follow and point at your target.

Having gotten this relaxed grip so that you can move the gun smoothly and freely in following a moving target, and having raised the gun to your face and shoulder so that there is no tension in your neck muscles in sighting it, the attitude of the rest of your body now becomes important. And here, when shooting at skeet targets or birds or any moving target, the left knee should be slightly bent. (For the left-handed shooter it's the right knee, of course, and the right hand on the fore-end.) I do not mean you should go into a crouch, but merely break the left knee. This will let your left hand lead your body without any restraint or tenseness. And the less tenseness, the better shot you will make.

The Follow-Through

As you move your body smoothly and freely, tracking a target or a bird to the left or to the right in a relaxed manner, another important principle comes up. Most beginners, when firing a shotgun, feel that that is the main event. And after pulling the trigger they quit, taking the gun down. Actually, pulling the trigger is only part of a process that was set in motion when you began to track the target. This process must continue if you're going to hit the target. In other words, you have to follow through. You have to

46 keep the gun swinging as though you had never pulled the trigger.

This is a difficult idea for a beginner, but it is an *absolute must*. If you think of pulling the trigger as the main event, then unconsciously, as the gun goes off, you will stop your swing. What happens then is this: Suppose you have raised your gun and are tracking a target, leading it by a foot, say, to make sure the shot charge hits. You establish this lead for a fraction of a second, pull the trigger, and quit as you do so. Well, in that moment that it takes the gun to fire, you will unconsciously have slowed down your gun swing. In doing this you will also have lost your foot lead. The shot charge will travel behind the target and you will have missed. This is the reason that you must follow through and keep the gun moving as though you had never pulled the trigger. This insures that the lead you have is the lead you still have when the shot charge leaves the barrel of your gun. If it was the correct lead to start with, you will break the target.

Three Types of Leads

On the skeet field, clay targets fly to and from you in the same manner birds fly—in all directions and at all angles. Some

Never forget safety. Keep receiver open and load the gun only when ready to shoot (left). Always keep barrel pointed toward the ground (right).

Braun shows that with a relaxed body and slightly bent left knee it is easy to move the gun through a wide arc without producing any tenseness

of these targets are shot dead on. Others require leads up to as much as four feet or so. By leads I simply mean that you must get your gun moving along with the target as you track it and then get the bead on your barrel out in front of the target by whatever amount, or lead, you will need to break it.

There are three methods of obtaining a lead. All of them are correct, and you will find many fine shooters using each of them. The first of these is called the swing-through system. In this system you start the gun moving with the target, but initially the bead is behind the target. Then the swing of the gun is accelerated so that the bead swings through the target and then pulls out ahead of it. As the bead crosses the target the trigger is pulled. But since the bead is swinging through the target and pulling out ahead of it, the gun is actually pointed somewhat ahead of the target at the time the shot charge leaves the muzzle. This, of course, is your lead. The faster the swing-through, the greater the lead provided by this method. It is obvious that a follow-through is an absolute must with this system, for without it no lead would be obtained, or only a portion of it.

The second method of getting a lead is to start with your bead

or restriction in the muscles of the body. This kind of smooth, relaxed swing is essential in moving with targets and also in following through.

more or less right on the target and then pull out ahead of it until the right lead is obtained. This system also requires split-second timing in firing the gun, for there is obviously only a moment when you will have the proper lead, and the trigger must be pulled at exactly that instant. Otherwise you will either have too little or too much lead, or else you'll be waving your gun barrel around. This requirement makes this system a bit tricky, also. But as I have said, many fine shooters use it with great success. Like all systems, a follow-through is essential. If you fail to follow through, you will be altering the smoothness of the pull-ahead method.

The third type of lead is called a maintained lead. This is the one I use, because I find it is the easiest and simplest of the three. With this system, you start your gun moving ahead of the target to begin with, and you keep it there as you raise the gun to your face and shoulder. Then, with your bead slightly ahead of the target, you merely adjust the lead to what that particular target requires, fire, and be sure to follow through. The moment you see you have the correct lead, you *must* fire. There is always the temptation to track the target too long in trying to make sure of your lead so you get a hit. But you simply cannot do this. If **49** you do, your muscles will begin to tense and your swing will slow down. Then you'll lose your lead and it will be a wasted shot. It is absolutely essential to remember that you haven't got time to double-check your lead except for a fraction of a second. If you do, you'll almost certainly miss the target. And again, don't forget to follow through.

Tracking with the Eyes

One very important matter in leading targets concerns where the shooter is actually looking. Always concentrate your gaze on the target or the bird you're shooting, and *not* on the bead of your gun. The bead should be used as a reference point only when obtaining your lead. A simple illustration will show you how this works.

Stand about four feet in front of a mirror and extend one arm out toward the mirror with your thumb sticking up. Let your thumb represent the bead on the barrel of your shotgun. Now look at your nose in the mirror, and let this be the target or bird. Put your thumb right on the nose, keeping your gaze concentrated on your nose in the mirror. You will find that you will see your thumb, even though you are concentrating on your nose. Now move your thumb a few inches to the right, while keeping your gaze on your nose. You are now leading your nose-target. And you will find that you can still see your thumb, even though you are looking at your nose, but only as a kind of reference point. While watching your nose, move your thumb farther out and then closer in. You will see that you constantly gauge the distance between your target and your reference point, while concentrating your gaze on the target. This is the way you should shoot. Always look right at the target, and let your bead be a reference point only.

In shooting, it is best to keep both eyes open at all times. However, this rule does not apply in one condition. Everybody has a master eye, that is, either the left eye or the right eye dominates. They cannot both be of equal strength. Punch a hole about the size of a quarter in the middle of a newspaper. Extend the paper at arm's length in front of you, concentrating your gaze on the hole. Quickly and smoothly draw the paper to your face. When it arrives, you will find that one of your eyes is looking directly through the hole, while the other is blocked by the newspaper. The eye that can see through the hole is the master eye. Normally, the right eye will be the master eye for a right-handed shooter, and the left eye will dominate for the left hander. However, if you shoot right-handed, and your left eye is your master eye, then you cannot keep both eyes open when shooting. In fact, it might be best to switch to left-handed shooting, if possible, so as to take advantage of both eyes.

Control and Concentration

Now we come to that most important fundamental of all, the one I touched on in the beginning: control. This is the most critical principle you will have to master if you are going to perfect your shooting. It is also the most difficult. This is *the* factor in championship shooting, of course. There just isn't any other. You can have the equipment, know-how, desire and everything else, but if you don't have control, you will never make a champion, either in this sport or in any other. You must forget the other shooter, distracting noises, conversation, how many straight you've shot or have left to shoot, or anything else that will take your mind off the business at hand. It is absolutely essential to improving your shooting, even if you're not out to win championships.

I will try to describe what control and concentration mean. When you come up to a station at skeet, or when you flush a bird in the field, there are certain simple things you must do to hit that target or that bird. You have to raise your gun properly, your actions have to be relaxed and smooth, you have to know the lead you need, and as you fire you must remember to follow through.

Now that all seems pretty simple—and it is. Yet it is exactly this simplicity that creates the problem of control. Ideas pop into your head from every conceivable direction. You can be about to shoot when you are reminded of something. Or suppose you are aware of how well somebody else is doing in the tournament. This information pops back into your head just as you are about to

The fore-end should be held in a light manner—like a handful of eggs (left). The barrel can then be pointed as easily as a finger (right).

call for the target. Popping up at that point, it is a distraction. Then you have your own self to contend with. You know perfectly well how many targets you have broken and how many more there are to break. If you think about that, that too becomes a distraction. These are the things that make control and concentration so difficult to master. The problem is not to do what you are doing. The problem is to shut out of your mind the great variety of things that can intrude and distract you.

For this reason, you have to shoot targets one at a time. If you start thinking about the target *after* the next one, or the target after that, you're in trouble. Nobody can break 25 straight, or 10 straight or 100 straight, until he has done just one thing—break the next target. I have trained myself to the point where, whether I'm shooting practice or a national tournament, each target I shoot is the most important I will ever shoot for the rest of my life. I have taught myself to shoot this way because it is the only way I know of really to concentrate on targets one at a time.

If you train yourself to do this—and I grant it is a hard lesson to learn—then you will break lots of 100 straights, win many tournaments, and have lots of fun. But, I warn you, it's not easy. It's the hardest, most concentrated work the

are many.

Habits

As you work on these fundamentals to improve ,
many fine points naturally arise. A few of these ma   1
mentioning. One thing that happens to shooters, and it   happen time after time, is that they work themselves into bad habits
without being aware of it. In 95 per cent of the cases it is a physical habit, a false or wrong move of some kind, that is causing the
shooter to miss. I have had many of the best shots in the world
come to me at different times and ask me to watch them shoot to
see if I can detect something they are doing incorrectly. In most
cases there is some little thing they are missing, and can consequently correct with no difficulty.

I have a personal friend with whom I've shot many times,
and in fact taught to shoot. It would hardly be an exaggeration
to say that when he started he was a Class ZZ shooter. Today he is
a Class A shooter in all four gauges, and on his way to AA status.
One of the particular troubles this friend has is that he counts
targets. I simply cannot make him realize that he must break only
the next target, which he can do and does do very well. But he
always wants to break 100 straight, and as he gets close to that
100 I can tell he's putting more and more effort into his shooting,
because I can see his muscles tighten up. He's trying to make
doubly sure of his leads and that's one of the best ways I know of
to miss targets.

I'd like to add another story about this same friend. It's a
bit off our subject, but illustrates something important. One day
he asked me what secret I had, that he didn't know, that enabled
me to break most of the targets most of the time. Now I had given
this friend every piece of knowledge I have in trying to help him
realize his desire to shoot well. So I thought the matter over and
told him that maybe I had not emphasized enough one thing that
I felt was very important in my own shooting. This is to start my
gun moving ahead of every target and not let any target get the   **53**

up on me. This gives me control of the gun point and enables me to obtain my lead in a smooth manner. Of course, I then fire and keep following through. So I said that if I had any secret left, it was perhaps only that I hadn't hit this point hard enough for him to emphasize it to himself.

After our conversation he went out and did as I said—and broke the most beautiful straight you ever saw. But I know it won't be long before he'll be worrying me again, thinking I've got still another secret up my sleeve. I haven't. I tell this story as an illustration of desire. This fellow has such a desire to break all the targets that he is continually working and striving, which is a virtue in this game. Consequently I am always glad to give him any assistance I can to help him break one or two more targets. I know he is in the process of making some really good scores when he starts talking to me this way. He is working mentally as hard as he can. If he can just stop counting, he'll be a double-A shooter in nothing flat.

As I have said, an experienced shooter can usually correct a bad habit, once it has been identified. The new shooter, however, who has recently broken a 25 and a 50 straight, is the fellow who really gets into trouble. In his own mind, after these feats, he has arrived. Then he starts kicking and stirring up the dust to really break a lot of targets. In doing this he begins to exert himself physically to try to improve his score. And as sure as the moon follows the sun he is going to begin having troubles. When his score drops down to 19s and 21s, and he's not breaking those 25s and 50s regularly, he begins to ask for advice. And believe me, you can find lots of advice.

If you have five or six people giving you advice, and you try everything you listen to, you're going to have five or six ways of shooting, plus your own. If you don't watch out, you'll have yourself in a real jam. When this happens you should stop and review your whole shooting procedure point by point, to see if you are really following all the fundamentals. You may have to watch a few fly by unbroken, but if you go over all the steps as if back at the beginning, you should be able to locate the difficulty.

54

Most people make the mistake of raising gun to their shoulder and then lowering their head, pressing cheek to the stock to sight along the gun.

Though I have said there is no such thing as an easy target at skeet, some are obviously more difficult than others. The most difficult are those at the three middle stations—3, 4 and 5. These stations require longer leads and a more positive follow-through. For the right-handed shooter, Low 4 and Low 5 are the most difficult targets. For a left-hander their equivalents, High 3 and High 4, are the most difficult. Often, because these stations are the most difficult, a shooter will become tense and stop his gun unconsciously on 3, 4 or 5, which is easy to do and which, of course, costs him the follow-through that is an absolute must on these stations. For these reasons you will find that most championships are lost on these stations. When targets are missed on 1, 2, 6, 7 and 8, you can put it down that the championship was given away.

The Middle Stations

There is an important fact about the middle stations on the skeet field that every shooter should know, and this is that they can vary from field to field. Slight changes in the way the traps are set can give you a different sight picture from one field to another. These changes can occur even on the same field, from one day to another. Therefore it is important to practice on a **55** strange field, even if you don't shoot any stations except 3, 4 and 5. You don't really have to worry about the remaining stations, as they will not change enough.

Crosswinds

Another variable that can affect these three middle stations is wind. A strong wind blowing right across the field, either from the high house to the low house or the low house to the high house, presents the shooter with a real problem. Consider the first condition for a moment, with the wind from the high to the low house. At these middle stations the targets are flying more or less at right angles to your field of view. For this reason they require the longest lead, as I have mentioned, and are the most difficult to hit. Now with the wind conditions mentioned, the high house targets will be travelling even faster than usual. Conversely, the low house targets will be unusually slow because they are headed into the wind.

A strong crosswind like this will present the most difficult conditions you will ever encounter on the skeet field, aside from the psychological factors. For here, two tough targets that normally travel at the same speed are now moving at quite different speeds. Though your leads will remain the same, your swing will have to be speeded up or slowed down accordingly. This can force you into a body movement you are not accustomed to on these stations. However, there is a simple mechanical adjustment you can make that will either slow or accelerate your swing and still leave you tracking the target in a normal fashion.

If you will simply extend your hand a little farther forward on the fore-end than you usually do, it will automatically slow down your swing. Conversely, if you move your hand a little back of your normal position, your swing will be accelerated. Also, since the target travelling with the wind will be getting out and away from you more quickly, you should change your gun-point position a bit. Here you move your barrel a little more toward Station 8, so that the target doesn't get the jump on you.

56 These crosswind conditions present problems on the other stations, too—for instance, in doubles on stations 1, 2, 6 and 7. Whichever the direction of the crosswind, I extend my hand to the rear slightly for doubles to give myself every advantage in breaking the fast target. In doing this, I also give myself a handicap, however, since this is really the wrong hand position for the slow target heading upwind. For I am now positioned for a fast swing instead of the slow swing the slow target really requires. To compensate, I have to be extra careful in pointing the gun to be sure I have a smooth movement and do not jerk the gun in any direction—an easy thing to do with a fast-swing fore-end position.

Triggering

Another little detail that can make the difference between 95 and 100 is having your finger placed correctly on the trigger. Holding your left thumb still, place the fleshy part of the first joint of your right index finger on the end of your thumbnail and press down. You will immediately see how much give there is to this soft part of your finger. Now move your thumbnail back to the crease in the first joint of your finger and repeat the experiment. Here, you will find, there is practically no give whatever.

The same thing is true when you place the fatty part of this first index finger joint on the trigger. When you press the trigger there is so much give in this soft tissue that you think you have pulled the trigger before all the pressure needed to pull it has actually been applied. Now slide your finger forward until the crease of the first joint is on the right-hand edge of the trigger. It should feel as if you had placed the edge of a dull knife against this crease. If you pull the trigger now, you will find that the gun will go off immediately, because there is no give to your finger. I have seen a lot of shooters extend their index fingers through the trigger guard and pull the trigger with the fatty part between the first and second joints. But this produces the same time lag.

This is just a little point, but a very important one. In that fraction of a second when you think you have the proper lead on a target, you have to pull the trigger. But if the gun does not go off at that instant, you will not have shot when you wanted to.

Using his thumb for a bead, Lee aims at the camera and then "leads" it to his right. His gaze remains fixed on camera representing target.

Lee shows that a shooter should concentrate on the target, seeing the bead only as a reference point out ahead of the target as he leads it.

This can give you the impression that you unconsciously delayed your shot and flinched.

Hand Position

Another point to take into account is the positioning of your hand on the fore-end of your gun, because this can affect the smoothness of your swing. For about 90 per cent of the population, this would be about halfway out on the fore-end. Guns are designed with that in mind. However, this doesn't hold for everybody. I happen to be six-feet-two and have long arms, but I hold my gun back of the center at the fore-end because I personally feel more comfortable with this position. In any event, the elbow should always be bent, so that you can swing the gun freely and easily without restriction. If your arm is extended too straight there will be a strain on it, and you will restrict your ease of movement. Thus an individual with short arms may find his best position to be about halfway back from the midpoint of the fore-end.

Team Shooting

I talked earlier about team shooting and pressure. As a pointer I would say the important thing to remember here is that *you,* personally, are not shooting the entire team score. There have been only a few occasions in history where an entire team broke the entire program. So it is not the shooters who are breaking the targets well and shooting a program clean that win a team championship. It is that poor fellow who has maybe dropped one or two targets and yet has the self-control to keep from coming unravelled, the control to keep going as best he can, who will pull the team through when the others are doing better than he is.

This becomes important in arranging a team. The best shot should be put in the Number 5 spot on the team, and the next best shot should be Number 1. The less experienced shooters should be in between. Number 1 is always under pressure. And if the first four members of the team are doing well, that anchor man, Number 5, is the boy who has got to carry the load. He must be

59

a shooter that can take the pressure and concentrate his mind on just that next target he has to break.

In shooting skeet today you are permitted to keep the butt of your shotgun on your shoulder as you call for the target. And many new shooters are taught this way. But I personally feel more relaxed holding the gun down and out, and any tenseness is fatal in skeet shooting. Furthermore, I don't hunt birds in the field with my gun to my shoulder, so I see no reason to shoot skeet that way.

As we turn to look at each of the skeet stations and how each target is shot, I would like you to note that there are two recognized ways of shooting a round of skeet. One is to shoot singles all the way from Station 1 through Station 8, and then shoot doubles at 1, 2, 6 and 7, with the optional target then shot at Station 7. However, in discussing the stations one by one, I feel it would be simpler to talk about both singles and doubles at 1, the same for 2, and so on around, ending up at 8. In this way we won't have to backtrack.

INTERNATIONAL SKEET

Whereas the regulations of the National Skeet Shooting Association permit a shooter to have his gun to his shoulder when calling for a target, the rules are quite different when it comes to competition in the Olympics and other international events. This is further reason for adopting a lower gun position, if a shooter expects to compete abroad. Under these international rules, when a shooter assumes his "Ready Position" to call for a target, some part of the gun butt must touch the top of his pelvic bone. This pelvic ridge, as it is called, can be felt through the flesh just below the belt line. Moreover, with the gun in this position some portion of the gun butt must be visible below the elbow when the shooter is viewed from the side by an official. For most shooters this latter condition would be fulfilled automatically when the gun is touching the pelvic ridge.

In the ready position for International skeet, the gun butt must touch the hip bone so that some portion of it is visible below shooter's elbow.

There is another important difference in the international rules, which concerns the variable release of targets. In the United States today, targets are released from the trap house immediately as the shooter calls for them. In international competition, however, the release time varies from instant release to as much as a three-second delay. This is accomplished by timers, which can release a target at any time up to three seconds after the shooter has called for it.

Both these international rules make breaking targets tough on the shooter. These same rules applied to U. S. skeet shooting at one time, but through the years gradual changes have been made. Today's shooters need not drop the stock at all prior to calling for the target, and the targets are released as soon as they are called for. Because of these rules changes, setting records today is much easier than it used to be.

NO LEAD

STATION
1

X In ready position, gun points here
Location of target when gun is fired
* Where gun points at instant of fire
— Path of the target
— Line of fire
--- Follow-through along target arc

At High 1, gun is held at 30° angle and gaze is elevated 15° above. Tape shows feet at 45° angle to trap house.

STATION
1

❝ THE FIRST OF TWENTY-FIVE SHOTS,
ALL OF WHICH TAKE A GREAT AMOUNT OF
MENTAL AND PHYSICAL CONTROL **❞**

■ Standing at Station 1, directly in front of the high house, your first concern will be body and foot position. This will be true of the other skeet stations as well. You can obtain the position I use at this station if you stand here with your back to the high house, face Station 8 squarely, and then turn your body 45 degrees toward the right. With your feet parallel and squared off in this new position, a line across your toes will make a 45° angle with a line from Station 8 to the high house. Now bend, or break, your left knee slightly, and place your gun stock to your face and shoulder. You will see the ease and flexibility this stance affords.

With this foot and body position you can shoot both the high house target and the low house target without any change in your stance. This becomes

65

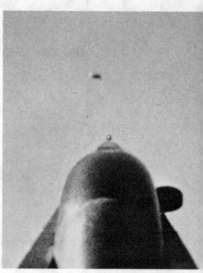

In camera-gun sequence, lead marker indicates zero lead (left). Then

important in shooting doubles, when both targets are in the air at the same time. In shooting doubles you will not have time to reposition your feet for the second shot. Therefore you want a position that will work correctly for both houses.

After obtaining a correct foot and body position, your next concern is how the gun is held and pointed, when to start the gun movement, and where to look for the target before calling for it.

For the high house target, move the stock of your gun out and down from your shoulder and face. Note that it is moved *out* and down, and not just *down* from the face. For a normal target, hold the gun down and out so that it is pointed at about a 30° angle in the air. The bead on the barrel is held on the line of flight the target will take as it flies out over your head and on toward a point about

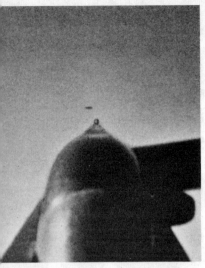

target appears, sails to area where gun is pointing and is shot dead on.

12 to 18 feet out from Station 8. Direct your gaze to a point about 15 degrees higher than the bead on the barrel. With an elevated gaze, you can still see your bead as a reference point—but you can also pick up the target quicker, since it will be coming from behind.

Now settle your body in a physically alert position, and call for the target. The moment it appears in your elevated view, raise the gun stock to your face smoothly and quickly, with your shoulder in position to receive the butt end of the stock without any forward or downward movement of the face. The moment the target settles on the front bead, fire without hesitation.

So look at high house 1 as a simple target and a straight-on shot. But you have to watch two things. Occasionally you will have an extra-high target, or a target that will dive under the path of a regulation target. If you find you have high targets to deal with, raise the bead of your gun a bit higher than 30 degrees. If you have a sinking target, lower the bead a little.

Whatever the conditions at high house 1, remember this: As you watch the target settle on your reference point, which is the bead on the front of your barrel, fire. If you don't fire at that moment, you're going to be moving the gun suddenly and tracking instead of simply raising it naturally and smoothly. If you get to tracking, you may very well miss it.

For the low house target at this station keep the same body and foot position. Move the gun out and down as before, but into a new position. This time the bead of the gun is directed toward a point about two-thirds of the way from the target intersection area near Station 8 back toward the low house. The reason the bead is placed out along the flight path of the target is that you're going to have to lead this target, so you'll have to be prepared to keep ahead of it. Here you want to position the bead a bit *under* the line of flight the target will take. The reason for this is that the target is coming from quite far off. You don't want to obscure your vision of it—which could happen if the muzzle of the gun were held too high. So put your bead in the suggested position and call for the target, watching the trap mouth as you do so.

Ordinarily, in obtaining a lead, you start the gun moving as the target appears, raise it to the face and shoulder, and then adjust your lead. However, the incomers on the end stations, 1, 2, 6 and 7, present a somewhat different situation. These targets will be traveling nearly all the way across the field before they reach the area where you want to break them, i.e. a point about two-thirds of the way from Station 8 back toward the house where you are waiting. You should break them at this two-thirds point because, when it comes to shooting doubles, this is about the point where you will have obtained the correct lead for your second target. So you should shoot the incomers on singles as you will shoot them on doubles, to develop a uniform shooting habit for all incomers. The more your shooting is simplified, the better your scores will be. Thus, if you start your gun moving with these incoming targets and then immediately begin raising it to your face and shoulder, you will be in a position to adjust your lead and fire long before the target is where you want to break it.

To avoid this, you start the gun moving normally with the target, and a little in front of it, but you do not begin to raise the gun until the target has reached the area of Station 8. In other words, **69**

10-12"

X In ready position, gun points here   Location of target when gun is fired
✳ Where gun points at instant of fire   Path of the target
— Line of fire   -- Follow-through along target arc

you act as though the Station 8 area were actually the trap house on all incomers. When the target reaches that area, then raise the gun to your face. Adjust your lead to about 10 or 12 inches for a fraction of a second, fire and follow through. With this procedure you will actually break the incomer where you want to, two-thirds of the way from 8 to the house where you are waiting, without having to hang on to your lead. Moreover, you will also be using the same timing on these incomers as you use on the outgoing targets, so that your raising and firing movements will be uniform around the field.

When you have obtained your 10 to 12 inch lead and have pulled the trigger, keep your gun moving in the direction the target was flying as though you had never pulled the trigger. This

71

Same foot position is used for the low house. Gun point
is 2/3 of the way from target intersection to low house.

 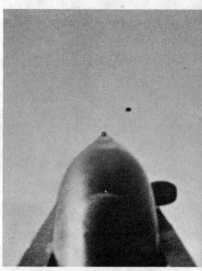

Lead marker specifies 1-foot lead, camera-gun swings along ahead of

follow-through is a *must* at every station. Even though Low 1 *looks* like an easy target, there's no easy target at skeet.

When it comes to doubles at this station, you must have in mind the fact that there is really no such thing as doubles. What counts is what happens now. If you're thinking about the second target and miss the first, then you'll miss your doubles. The important thing is to think of doubles as though you had two singles in the air at the same time. So think about the first target first, and *then* turn to the second target.

In shooting doubles, you maintain the foot and body position already described. You position the gun for the first target, which will be High 1, just as you did on singles. If you shoot High 1 as you did in singles, you will break this target in the area of

72

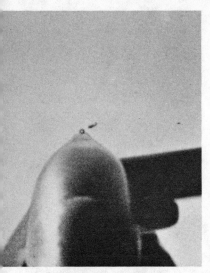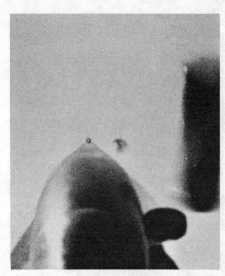

target, lead is adjusted and target is broken as gun follows through.

Station 8. After—I repeat *after*—you have seen the target break, then start your barrel moving gradually back toward the high house. Since the low house target will have arrived in the vicinity of Station 8 at about the same time the high house target got there, and since this is where you will have broken the high house target, you should have no trouble in picking up the low house target visually as you start your swing back toward the high house. In the course of your swing you establish your lead of from 10 to 12 inches and then break the low house target about two-thirds of the way from Station 8 back to the high house station, just as you did on singles. Keep your gun to your face and shoulder, keep the muzzle swinging as though you had never pulled the trigger, and you should have no trouble breaking both singles and doubles at Station 1. **73**

IN THE FIELD

Since one of the principal reasons for shooting skeet is to improve a shooter's field shooting, it is interesting to see just what type or kind of field shot each station and each target at skeet might represent. High house 1, for instance, is like a hunter in a blind when a duck or dove flies over him from behind and heads off into the distance just as the shooter spots him. The comparison is quite close in another respect, too—the speed of the target. Skeet targets travel at about 45-55 miles per hour, which is a bit less than the speed of most ducks flying downwind, but gives a good comparative shot.

Low house 1 applies to ducks and doves also, in this case representing birds flying toward the shooter at a slight angle and a low altitude, as though they had just taken off from a pond or **74** water hole.

Photo-diagram suggests a typical High 1 type of shot in the field, with bird flying over and away from hunter.

In a Low 1 field shot, bird flushes from cover, climbs as it approaches hunter and then veers off to his left.

STATION

2

X In ready position, gun points here
Location of target when gun is fired
* Where gun points at instant of fire
— Path of the target
— Line of fire
– – – Follow-through along target arc

In correct position for the high house, a line across toes intersects path to 8 at 90°. Gun point is the same.

STATION

2

■   As at Station 1, you have only a single foot position for both targets, since you're going to shoot doubles at this station also. Standing at this station with your feet parallel and your toes squared off, a line drawn across your toes should make a 90° angle with the path from the high house to Station 8.

With your feet in this position, bend the left knee slightly. Then extend your gun down and out, so that it is pointing in the same direction as the line across your toes, directly into the path between the high house and 8. Place the bead on the line of flight the target will take from the high house. With your body physically alert, look directly at the trap mouth and call for your target.

The moment it appears, start your gun moving to the right, keeping it slightly ahead of the target   **79**

Marker shows a 1-1 1/2 foot required lead. Then target sails out as

and watching the target at all times. Simultaneously, you should be raising your gun to your face, to be backed up by your shoulder, which will be in a position to receive it without any extra movement of your body. While continuing to watch the target, you will also be able to see your bead, or reference point. Adjust your lead to about a foot or a foot and a half. The instant you see that lead, fire. Then keep moving the gun and keep pointing as though you had never pulled the trigger.

The high house target at this station is often thought of as a difficult target, as it appears to get away fast because you are so close to the trap house. This illusion can lead you into going after this target too quickly. If you do that, you will get too far ahead of it and have to stop your swing and fire. And if there is any hesitation in your swing, or any

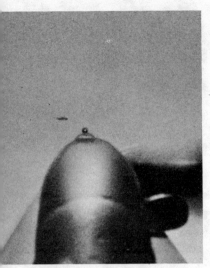

camera-gun maintains a lead ahead of it, adjusts lead, breaks target.

abrupt movement, you may miss the target.

Another point about High 2 is that you can shoot right at it and break it—*if* you follow through. But you will break it only with the forward edge of your shot pattern. I try to lead it by a foot or a foot and a half, which puts the target right in the middle of the pattern and gives me insurance in case I should slow my swing for any reason.

I've been asked by many shooters where I break High 2. You break any target except the incomers on 1, 2, 6 and 7 at the point where you obtain your correct lead. The moment you have your lead, allow just a *fraction of a second* to make sure and then pull the trigger. If you allow more time than that you will slow down your swing and, instead of making doubly sure, you may miss the target. The main thing is to make sure you have the right sight

2-2½'

X In ready position, gun points here   ▬▬ Location of target when gun is fired
✳ Where gun points at instant of fire   ▬▬ Path of the target
── Line of fire   ─ ─ Follow-through along target arc

picture of your lead before you pull the trigger, because it's not *where* you break the target but *whether* you break it that counts.

For the incomer at Station 2, the low house target, keep the same foot and body position as for the high house. With your left knee slightly bent, extend your gun down and out and place your bead about two-thirds of the way from Station 8 back to the low house. Be sure your bead is about a foot *under* the line of flight this target will take, instead of *on* it as for the high house. The reason for this is that this is a low-traveling target. If you start your gun too high, you can obscure the target as you raise the gun to your face.

Look at the trap mouth, call for the target, and the moment it appears start your gun moving along

Retaining same foot position for Low 2, gun point is 2/3 of the way from 8 to low house and under target path.

With a 2-2 1/2 foot lead indicated by the lead marker, the camera-gun

ahead of it, raising the gun stock to your face only after the target has reached the area of Station 8. Now adjust your lead to about 2 or 2½ feet, fire, and follow through as though you had never pulled the trigger. You will break this target as you did the incomer on Station 1, about two-thirds of the way from 8 back to the high house.

We now come to doubles on Station 2. And as I have said earlier, there is no such thing as doubles—there are only two single shots in the air at the same time. You *must* shoot your targets one at a time, and not think about the second target while you're shooting the first one.

Keeping the left knee slightly bent, point your gun straight into that line from Station 8 to the high house, put your bead on the line of flight of the target, and call for it. The moment it appears start

swings along ahead of incomer, gets its lead, and breaks the target.

your gun moving smoothly, bring it to your face and shoulder, and the instant you see your lead of a foot or a foot and a half and check it for a fraction of a second, pull the trigger and follow through. You will probably break this target a little before or around Station 8 and the low house target will be in just about this same area at the same time.

As soon as you see the high house target break, start your gun moving smoothly back toward the high house, while looking into space to pick up the low house target. It should be readily apparent in this same area. After picking it up, adjust your lead to 2 or 2½ feet, fire, and follow through. You will find that you have broken this target about two-thirds of the way from 8 back to the high house, which was the reason for breaking it there on singles.

85

IN THE FIELD

There are a number of common field situations which present a shooter with a high house type of shot at Station 2. Think of yourself as a hunter walking along with a hedgerow or a row of trees to your left. You come to the end of the row, at which point a grouse or dove is seen flying out from this cover at a slight angle away from the hunter. Or you could be watching from some natural cover, or from a blind, when a duck approached your position from behind and then flared off at a slight angle to the left as it spotted you. You would then have an almost straightaway shot at the bird as it got some distance from your shooting position.

Low 2 is again most likely to be a duck or dove shot. Here the bird would be flying toward you and, on seeing you, would veer off slightly to its right but continue on past your position.

A High 2 shot in a hunting situation suggests a bird emerging from cover to shooter's left and at an angle.

In a Low 2 situation, the bird takes off from in front of shooter and heads his way at an angle to his left.

4-4½′

STATION
3

X In ready position, gun points here
Location of target when gun is fired
※ Where gun points at instant of fire
— Path of the target
— Line of fire
--- Follow-through along target arc

For high house, line across toes extends to a point 8-9 feet out from it. Gun point: 2/3 distance from 8 to house.

STATION

3

66 **THE THREE DIFFICULT MIDDLE
STATIONS REQUIRE A LONGER LEAD AND A
MORE POSITIVE FOLLOW-THROUGH** 99

■ Now come the three middle stations on the field
—3, 4 and 5. These are the most difficult because they
require a longer lead and a more positive and as-
sured follow-through. My lead at each of these stations, for both the high and the low house, is from
4 to 4½ feet. However, both the low and high house
targets on these middle stations can be broken with
slightly over a three-foot lead. I add this extra
foot or foot and a half as insurance, so that if I
slow up my follow-through I will still have something going for me to try and get a piece of that
target.

Almost invariably, if you miss these targets it
is because you are shooting behind them. There are
two chief reasons why this happens. One is a failure
to follow through properly. The other is a failure

to obtain the proper lead on firing. An inadequate follow-through may be caused by tenseness or by a physical effort to shoot the target a little too fast. Too little lead is due to the shooter's failing to check his lead for a fraction of a second before pulling the trigger.

For the high house target, parallel your feet and square your toes once more. Place your feet in a position so that a line across the toes would extend to a point about 8 or 9 feet out from the high house toward Station 8. Use this same position for all three middle stations when shooting the high house. Now bend your left knee slightly, look directly at Station 8, and then estimate a point about two-thirds of the way from Station 8 back to the high house. That's the point from where you will start your gun and call for the target.

Extend the gun down and out toward this point, with the bead on the line of flight the target will take. Looking directly at the trap mouth, with your body relaxed but physically alert, call for your target. As it appears, start the muzzle of your gun moving along slightly in front of the target, at the same time raising the gun to your face and shoulder. Never take your eye off the target as you raise your gun. Remember, your bead is a reference point—it will be apparent to you while you are watching the target. Remember also not to jerk the gun stock to your face and shoulder. Move it up as smoothly and as swiftly as you can, without upsetting the direction of your gun point or the movement of your body.

After your gun is in firing position, and still moving, your bead should be slightly in front of the target. Now for just a fraction of a second, adjust your lead to between 4 and 4½ feet, pull the trigger immediately, and follow through as though you had never pulled the trigger.

For the low house target you have to change foot position, instead of using a single stance as on the end stations. On these three middle stations you must move your gun and body through too great an arc to maintain the same position for both houses. A new position is required for the low house that will let you move from the starting point to the end in a smooth, fast and relaxed manner. For Low 3, then, parallel your feet so that a line across the toes extends to a point about 10 to 12 feet to the left of Station 8 toward the high house. With the left knee slightly bent, look directly at 8 and then estimate a distance about two-thirds of the way from there back to the low house. This is the gun-point position for starting your swing.

Extend your gun down and out toward this point, with your bead six inches to a foot under the

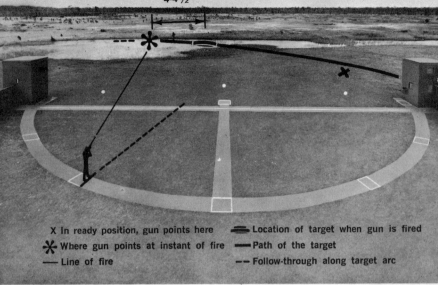

4-4½′

X In ready position, gun points here   ▰ Location of target when gun is fired
✱ Where gun points at instant of fire   ▬ Path of the target
— Line of fire   -- Follow-through along target arc

line of flight of the target, and settle your body in a relaxed, alert condition. Then look directly at the trap mouth and call for the target. The moment it appears, start your gun moving smoothly to the left and break this target exactly the same way you did on the high house, using the same lead.

Ordinarily a left-handed shooter will find High 3 the most difficult target on the skeet field. These middle stations are tough to begin with, and to the left-hander High 3 will appear to get out and away from him extremely fast. This, plus the need for a longer lead and an absolute follow-through on these stations, will make High 3 difficult for a southpaw. Comparably for the right-hander, the most difficult target on the middle stations will be Low 5, and for the same reasons.

For the low house, the toe-line extends to 10-12 feet to left of 8. Gun point is 2/3 of way from 8 to house.

IN THE FIELD

Both houses at all three of these middle stations are typically dove or duck situations, with birds flying more or less at right angles. This is also true of grouse. (Researchers have computed the average speed for unmolested grouse at 41 miles per hour.) Anyone who has ever hunted grouse knows that, more often than not, your dog or partner is going to flush a bird that flies at a direct right angle to you in the identical pattern of a skeet target from Stations 3, 4 or 5. It is true you won't often get a clear open shot like this on "old Ruff," but the lead required to stop him doesn't often vary from a skeet target on the middle positions. These shots are hard at skeet, and they're hard in the field, too. Having three of these middle stations to shoot at skeet provides you with a lot of good practice for some tough field shots.

When it is encountered in the field, a High 3 shot will be a bird flying across shooter's view and away from him.

Low 3 could be a duck or a dove taking off from hunter's right, gaining altitude, and flying slightly toward him.

4-4½'

STATION

4

X In ready position, gun points here
▬ Location of target when gun is fired
✳ Where gun points at instant of fire
━ Path of the target
── Line of fire
▬▬▬ Follow-through along target arc

Like High 3, toe-line hits a point 8-9 feet from the trap house, and gun point is 2/3 from 8 back to it.

STATION
4

THE MOMENT YOU HAVE THE PROPER LEAD—CHECK FOR JUST A FRACTION OF A SECOND—FIRE!

Before discussing Station 4, the second of the three middle stations, I would like to emphasize again the importance of shooting these difficult targets the moment you have the proper lead and have checked it for just a fraction of a second. This is tough for a new shooter to do, because these targets travel quite fast and are hard to lead correctly. And because they can be tracked all the way across the field at these stations, a new shooter will have a tendency to follow them or track them too long while he double-checks and rechecks his lead. This is fatal. If you attempt to hang on to a lead for any length of time, your body will become tense instead of moving in a relaxed and easy manner. When this happens, you can't help but slow down or stop your swing. We call this trying, or measuring, the shot.

Viewed from camera-gun, the lead marker reveals the long lead needed

It will cause you to miss many, many targets. You must force yourself to fire the gun the second you have your correct lead.

For the high house on Station 4, the foot position is the same as it was for High 3. A line across the toes will extend to a point about 8 or 9 feet out from the high house toward Station 8. Bend the left knee, look at 8, and then estimate a distance two-thirds of the way from there to the high house to get your gun starting position. Now put your bead on the line of flight of the target, look at the trap mouth, and call for your target. As it appears, start your gun moving to the right while raising it to your face and shoulder, get your lead of from 4 to 4½ feet, fire, and keep the gun moving and pointing as though you had never pulled the trigger.

If you get yourself into the habit of obtaining

on all middle stations: 4-4 1/2 feet. With this lead, target is broken.

the correct sight-picture of the targets on any one of these stations, then you have the right sight picture on all of them. For 3, 4 and 5 are exactly alike. So when you make a good shot, remember what you did and how you did it, record it in your mind—and then repeat it over and over and over.

The low house target is also like Low 3, with the line across the toes going to a point about 10 to 12 feet to the left of Station 8 toward the high house. Again you estimate your gun point about two-thirds of the way from 8 to the low house. Place your bead under the line of flight of the target, look at the trap mouth, and call for the target. The moment you see it, start your gun muzzle moving in front of it while raising your gun to your face. Obtain a lead of 4 to 4½ feet, check it for just that fraction of a second, fire, and keep moving your body as directed by

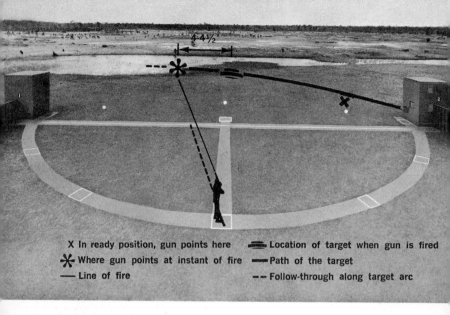

4 4½'

X In ready position, gun points here   ━━ Location of target when gun is fired
✳ Where gun points at instant of fire   ━━ Path of the target
── Line of fire   ─ ─ Follow-through along target arc

the hand that is pointing your barrel, so that there is no stop, no hesitation, and no jerk. Remember that a smooth, positive follow-through is an absolute must on these stations.

You have probably noticed that on all the high house targets except High 1, you place the bead of the barrel exactly on the line of flight of the target. The reason for this is that the high house target *is* a high target, and its movement is out and down. With this kind of flight path, all you have to do is follow along the line of flight with your bead and you will have no other adjustments to make except to obtain your lead. On the low house targets, however, the target comes from a low position and travels upward. If you start with your bead right on the line of flight of the low house target, it is easy

104

*Toe-line is same as for Low 3, 10-12 feet to left of
Station 8. So is gun point, 2/3 back from 8 to low house.*

With a 4-4 1/2 foot lead again indicated by the marker, the camera-gun

to block out your view of this target momentarily as you raise your gun. But you never want to lose sight of that target.

Another factor is involved here as well, which makes it important to keep the bead six inches or a foot under the line of flight of these low house targets. As the target appears and travels upward, there is a human tendency to start the gun moving in too much of a climb, in order to stay with the target. For this reason, you can pull up and over this target, thereby obscuring and losing track of it. Then you have to readjust your whole movement after the target has gotten too far toward Station 8—and in effect you are then making a completely new shot after the target is in the air. This is hard to do without a lot of experience, and that's why I keep my bead below the target. From this correct

maintains a long lead on its target, adjusts, and breaks the target.

starting position, you have the target in sight at all times and can smoothly swing with it, keeping it in view in relation to your reference point—the bead on your barrel.

Many times a shooter will only chip a target. And these chips can tell you something. When you see a chip fall off the front end of your target, be well satisfied. Know that you had plenty of lead and were a long way from missing it. However, when chips drop off the back end of your target, don't panic, but understand that either you didn't have enough lead or you didn't follow through properly. A part of the cure, of course, is to increase your lead slightly. But don't overdo it. And another important part of the cure is to make sure you are keeping your gun moving after you have pulled the trigger.

IN THE FIELD

On Station 3 we noted that the types of field shots represented by that station are really duplicated on Stations 4 and 5. There is no real difference. However, one thing worth noting at this point concerns the matter of leads. Skeet targets travel at about 45 to 55 miles per hour. The leads I am giving you are for targets at those speeds.

A number of researchers have computed the flight speeds of various unmolested game birds. It is impossible to say that these speeds are exact, but they constitute the best information to date.

Speeds are in miles per hour: dove—34; quail, prairie chicken, ruffed grouse, jacksnipe, mallard, black duck, spoonbill, pintail, wood duck, widgeon, gadwall—41; Canadian geese, brant—48; green-winged teal—79; blue-winged teal—89; canvasback—94.

High 4 represents one of the most difficult shots in the field, a fast-flying bird traveling across shooter's view.

Low 4 is an equally difficult field shot, with a bird rising from the shooter's right flying in front of him.

4-4½'

X In ready position, gun points here
— Location of target when gun is fired
✳ Where gun points at instant of fire
— Path of the target
— Line of fire
--- Follow-through along target arc

As at 4, toe-line extends to point 8-9 feet out from high house. Gun point is 2/3 distance from 8 to house.

STATION
5

❝❝ LOW 5, THE MOST DIFFICULT
TARGET ON THE SKEET FIELD, CAN MAKE
OR BREAK A RIGHTHANDED SHOOTER. ❞❞

■ This is the last of the three middle stations on the skeet field. Here you will have the same foot and body positions as you did for stations 3 and 4. For the high house target at Station 5, stand with your feet parallel as always. The line across your toes will extend toward a point about 8 or 9 feet out from the high house in the direction of Station 8. As before, you find your gun-point position by looking at Station 8 and then letting your gaze move from there back toward the high house to a point about two-thirds of the way from 8 to the house. Hold your gun down and out, look at the trap mouth and call for your target.

The moment the target appears, start your gun moving immediately along the line of flight of the target and a bit ahead of it, at the same time smoothly and quickly raising your gun to your face. Then adjust your lead to from 4 to 4½ feet. Once you have this lead, and have taken the barest fraction of a second to make sure of it, pull the trigger immediately and follow on through. Remember, a positive follow-through is an absolute must on Stations 3, 4 and 5.

For the low house target, the foot position is changed just as it was on the previous two stations. With your feet parallel, a line across your toes should extend to a point about 12 feet to the left of Station 8. For your gun-point position, look at Station 8 and then let your gaze move to a point about two-thirds of the way from 8 back to the low house. Extend your gun down and out, look at the trap mouth and call for the target. Start your gun moving smoothly ahead of it the moment it appears, while at the same time raising the gun to your face. Adjust your lead to 4 to 4½ feet with a moment's check, fire, and follow through.

To me, Low 5 is the hardest target on the skeet field. That's for a right-hand shooter, of course. It presents basically the same problem to a right-hander that High 3 does to the left-handed shooter. Low 4 isn't much easier. At Low 5 the right-handed shooter is getting closer to the low trap house. The target flies out at what appears to be an unusually **114** fast clip as seen from this vantage point. As a result, the shooter feels he has to hurry. In doing this, smoothness and follow-through are neglected, and the shooter actually fire's before he is ready. Low 5 is the most-often-missed target on the skeet field. It is this shot, more than any other, with which right-handers win or lose their tournaments.

Here are two illustrations of the importance of the foot positions I have prescribed for these middle stations. Standing at Station 5, parallel your feet for the high house shot so that a line across your toes will extend directly to Station 1, instead of the prescribed point of about 8 or 9 feet out in front of it. Now place the gun to your face, backed up by your shoulder, and start turning to the right as though you were tracking this high house target. But make your swing very slow.

As your gun point reaches the area of Station 8 you will begin to feel a tenseness extending down from your right shoulder, through your waist, and on into your right leg. And as you continue your swing toward the low house, this restriction and tension in your body will grow even greater.

Conversely, if the line across your toes is farther out toward Station 8 than I have suggested—say two-thirds of the way out toward 8 from the high house—when you get set for your gun point, you will be twisting back toward the high house. Your body will then be under stress.

4-4½'

X In ready position, gun points here   ▬ Location of target when gun is fired
✳ Where gun points at instant of fire   ▬ Path of the target
▬ Line of fire   -- Follow-through along target arc

In this same fashion, you can demonstrate to yourself the correctness of the low house foot position by letting the line across your toes run considerably more toward the high house, or letting it run directly to Station 8. If you swing your body slowly to the left in either of these positions, as though you were leading a target, you will find that your body is under tension, just as it was in the first two illustrations of the wrong foot positions.

From these illustrations you can see why your foot position, your body position, and your gun-point position are all important—particularly so on these middle stations, where nothing must be off. If they are incorrect, you will get into a situation in which your body will become tense and you will then have a tendency to muscle your gun.

116

Line across toes extends to point 10-12 feet to the left of 8. Gun point: 2/3 the distance from 8 to low house.

IN THE FIELD

Since there are three middle stations on the skeet field, a shooter gets six shots at the toughest targets of all in a single round of this sport. These are the crossing shots that require a longer lead and a complete and positive follow-through. Because these are the most difficult field shots as well, this fact about skeet makes it particularly helpful in improving your field shooting. This becomes important when you consider actual field conditions. Here footing may be rough, and there may be no time to get a proper body position on a suddenly flushing bird. Under such circumstances, the remaining elements—a smooth, relaxed swing, the right lead, and a positive follow-through—become critical. So the more practice a shooter has had, the greater chance he will have of downing a bird **118** under difficult conditions in the field.

High 5 is another difficult field shot, with the bird flying across in front of the shooter and toward him.

Low 5 is similar, but with the bird getting the jump on shooter from low cover, and traveling to his right.

2-2½'

On this station, a line across the toes extends directly to Station 8. Gun point is 2/3 distance from 8 to high house.

STATION

6

IF YOU CAN BREAK TARGETS AT BOTH HOUSES AT STATION 2, THEN THERE'S NO REASON FOR YOU TO MISS HERE.

Station 6 is really a mirror image of Station 2. The leads are identical. The outgoing target will require a 1 or 1½ foot lead, and the incomer a 2 or 2½ foot lead so you will shoot them with the same leads as you did on 2. The only differences are in foot and body position, and the gun point on the low house.

The correct foot position for both houses is to stand with your feet parallel, so that a line across your toes will extend directly to Station 8. In singles, the high house target will be shot first. Load your gun, look at Station 8, and then locate that point about two-thirds of the way from 8 to the high house. This is your gun start. With the left knee slightly bent, hold your gun down and out and put the bead on the line of flight the target will take, ex-

123

tending the gun toward the start point. Look at the trap mouth, relax, call for your target, and the moment it appears start your gun moving slightly ahead of it. Raise the gun to your face and shoulder when the target reaches Station 8. Now adjust your lead to about 2 to 2½ feet and break the target about two-thirds of the way from 8 back to the low house, the same place where you will break it on doubles.

For Low 6, body and foot positions remain the same. However, the gun-point position differs from the comparable position on Station 2. For High 2, (which is like Low 6), the gun was pointed directly into the line between the high house and Station 8, so as to make a 90° angle with it. For Low 6 you do the same thing, but then you advance the gun point two or three feet out toward 8. The reason for this is that a right-handed shooter tends to move his gun to the left faster and more abruptly than he does to the right. But with the gun point a bit farther out, he won't be in such a rush, and this will slow down and smooth out the swing and eliminate any tendency to go after the target too fast. If you rush a target, you can end up with your gun too far ahead of the target and have to stop your swing and wait. This eliminates the follow-through. Another thing that also happens when you move too quickly on **124** this target is that you can shoot over it. For the left-handed shooter, the situation is exactly the opposite. He exhibits this same tendency on High 2, and so should advance his gun point the same two or three feet from the high house toward station 8.

With your gun down and out and in position for Low 6, be sure the bead is at least 6 inches under the line of flight of the target. And be sure you are relaxed and alert. Then look directly into the trap mouth, call for the target, and the moment it appears start your barrel moving slightly ahead of it, at the same time raising your gun. Obtain a 1 or 1½ foot lead for a fraction of a second, fire, and follow through as though you had never pulled the trigger. Remember, this lead is insurance. You can actually break this target by firing directly at it, but only if you have an absolutely positive follow-through. But this lead gives you a virtual certainty of hitting the target, provided that you follow through.

In doubles at this station, we reverse the order we shot the targets in singles, shooting the low house first. Again, there is no such thing as doubles. There are only two singles in the air at the same time. Keeping the same foot and body position, load two shells in your gun and prepare to shoot the low house target first. Eliminate everything from your mind except the low house target. With the gun-point directly in the line between the low house and

X In ready position, gun points here   ▬ Location of target when gun is fired
✳ Where gun points at instant of fire   ▬ Path of the target
▬ Line of fire   -- Follow-through along target arc

Station 8, but advanced a few feet, place the bead below the line of flight of the target, look at the trap mouth and call for the target. As it appears, start your gun moving smoothly in front of it, bring it up to firing position, get your 1 or 1½ foot lead, fire and follow through, making sure you see that target break down your barrel before you think of anything else.

You will have broken this target before or around the area of Station 8, and at the same time the high house target will be coming into that same area, just as with doubles on Station 2. Look into space to pick up this target and, at the same time, start your gun moving back toward the low house. Once you find the target, adjust your lead to 2 to 2½ feet, fire and follow through.

*Foot position remains same for low house. Gun point
is directly into path to 8, but advanced a yard to 8.*

IN THE FIELD

Upland game hunters can expect a game shot similar to high house 6 many times through the course of a season. Quail, pheasants or partridge flushed by a dog or another person will often fly toward another hunter in this flight pattern.

If you have ever hunted woodcock, you know that they are likely to flush in any direction. There is, however, one habit woodcocks have that can be a great help to the hunter. They often angle out of an alder thicket away from the gunner, usually in pretty much of a hurry. Woodcock shooting can be as fast as gunning ruffed grouse, but at least the bird will fly away from you. Low house 6 comes close to duplicating the flight of a woodcock. Shooters who consistently break this target on the skeet field generally get their share of timber-doodlers, too.

A High 6 field shot is a lot like a Low 2 shot, except that the bird has a greater altitude as it veers off.

In the field, Low 6 is like bird taking off from cover to the hunter's right and flying away while veering off.

10-12"

X In ready position, gun points here
▬ Location of target when gun is fired
✳ Where gun points at instant of fire
▬ Path of the target
——— Line of fire
--- Follow-through along target arc

Here, a line across the shooter's toes extends directly toward 8, and gun point is 2/3 the distance from 8 to the high house.

STATION

7

HIGH 7 IS WITHOUT A DOUBT THE EASIEST OF ALL SKEET SHOTS—BUT DON'T COUNT YOUR CHICKENS.

On Station 7, as on 1, 2 and 6, we have the same foot and body positions for both houses. Here, a line across your toes will extend directly to Station 8. In taking this position, stand as far back from the trap mouth as possible. Occasionally a target will fly out broken and slash against the side of the trap mouth, throwing fragments that can cut you or mar your gun.

Here, as at Station 6, the high house target comes first. Position yourself with your knee bent and your gun held slightly down and out, and get your gun start position. This will be two-thirds of the way from the place the targets cross out beyond Station 8, back to the high house. Note that here I have said the crossing point of the targets, rather than Station 8 itself. This is the actual two-thirds

133

distance you want, from the crossing point to whatever house you're shooting. When you are shooting the middle stations, 3, 4 and 5, you might as well look at Station 8 and then gauge the two-thirds distance from there, because the crossing point is practically behind 8 anyway, looking at it from that angle. But when you get around toward 7, this is not the case. In fact, at 7 you see Station 8 in line with the high house, and no two-thirds estimate is possible. So, as you come around from the middle stations, you have to take this into consideration.

Having prepared yourself, look at the trap mouth, call for your target and start your gun moving along ahead of the target. When the target is in the vicinity of Station 8, raise your gun to your face and shoulder, adjust your lead to 10 to 12 inches and break this target about two-thirds of the way from 8 back to the low house, where you will break it on doubles.

For the low house target, stand with your gun down and out as always and with your bead aimed at the point of intersection of the targets, out beyond Station 8. And as with all low house targets, your bead should be six inches to a foot under the line of flight the target will take. Here, as at High 1, you cannot watch the trap mouth for the target to emerge. You have to set yourself to pick it up in flight. Simply look out over your gun barrel toward the point where the targets intersect. When you call for this target, you will notice it quickly as it comes into view. Then simply raise your gun to your face, to be backed up by your shoulder, and as you see this target settle on your bead, fire.

It is important here not to move your gun abruptly or with a jerk, as it is very easy to shoot over this target. The reason for putting the bead under the line of flight of the target is that you want to keep the target always in view. If you raise your gun so that you are right on the line of flight of this target and see it on the bead of your barrel, you should shoot it right then and there. But if at that moment the target should duck from a sudden puff of wind or some such, you will shoot right over the top of it. However, if your bead is a bit below the target and this happens, you can shoot the moment the target is on your bead, even if you're not completely ready. And you should get a piece of it, anyway.

For doubles at Station 7, keep the same body and foot positions. But now shoot the low house target first, as you did on 6. Extend your gun down and out, relax and be alert, and place your bead below the flight of the low house target. Looking out toward the Station 8 intersection, call for the target. As it comes into view, raise your gun smoothly. Fire as the target settles on your front

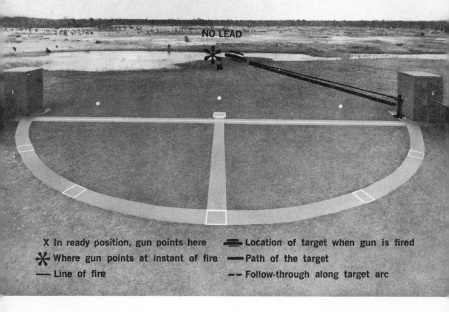

NO LEAD

bead, and hold until you see it break down the barrel. Then start moving your gun back toward the low house while looking for the high house target, which should be in the vicinity of Station 8. As you pick it up, adjust your lead to about 10 or 12 inches and fire. Be sure, and I mean be *sure,* even though you know this is a floater and is right on top of you, that you follow through. Don't relax until you have seen the target break. *Then* relax. After having shot doubles on Station 7, you will have one of your original twenty-five shells left. This is your optional. If you have not missed a single target, according to the current skeet rules you can shoot this optional at any target on the field. I never have shot—and I never will shoot—any target as the optional except High 7.

*With same foot position, also needed for doubles, the gun
point is toward target intersection out from Station 8.*

IN THE FIELD

An incoming bird, whether it be a greenhead, mallard, ducking snipe or a zooming grouse, is a tough shot under any conditions. Chances are, due to a combination of excitement, heavy clothes and just plain "bird fever," you missed him because of too short a lead or by stopping your gun—the same reason you missed the target at High 7.

Somebody once said, "A pheasant flying straight away is a hard shot because it looks so easy." There's truth in the statement. Every hunter, regardless of the type of bird he hunts, can expect a good percentage of his birds to fly dead straight away from him. The majority of the time he'll be right on target, but every once in a while he will raise his head off the stock just a little before he squeezes the trigger. The result of this is quite generally a very grateful pheasant.

A High 7 shot in the field is like a bird cruising in toward the hunter and then drifting off to his right.

A Low 7 shot relates to a bird bursting out from nearby cover, taking off in a straight line away from shooter.

NO LEAD

STATION
8

X In ready position, gun points here

━━ Location of target when gun is fired

✳ Where gun points at instant of fire

━ Path of the target

── Line of fire

- - - Follow-through along target arc

Here the foot position is the same as for Station 7, and gun point is 6-7 feet out along the path of the target.

STATION
8

❞❞ IT IS IMPERATIVE THAT YOU
FIRE THE MOMENT YOU SEE THE TARGET IS
COVERED WITH YOUR FRONT BEAD. ❞❞

■ This is the last station on the skeet field. To a
new shooter this appears to be a most difficult shot,
because you are right in the middle of the field between the two houses. This station puts you twice
as close to the traps as any others, so that when the
targets fly out they are on you in nothing flat. Actually this is not as difficult a shot as it first appears.
It is really a coordinated spot shot, in which you
simply raise the gun smoothly and quickly and
shoot as soon as you have covered the target. There
isn't time to do anything more. If you simply do
what I have just said—and do it properly—and follow through, Station 8 targets will be easy because
you have a big pattern of shot to break them with.

The high house target is your first shot, and
while waiting your turn I suggest that you stand   **143**

This is a dead-on shot with no lead, and the camera-gun picks up the

slightly to the rear of the person shooting this station, so you can watch the path of the target, its line of flight, and the movement of the shooter in front of you. This will help you get into the rhythm and timing it takes to break this target.

When your turn comes, your foot and body positions will be exactly the same as they were for Station 7. With your feet parallel, a line across your toes would run directly to the high house. Bend your left knee slightly, extend your gun down and out, and make sure you place your bead on the line of flight this target will take. This is why I suggest that you watch the shooters ahead of you, so you will have a clear idea of this target path. Your bead should be about 6 or 7 feet out from the trap mouth, and on this line of flight. Now you are ready to call for the target. Look at the trap mouth, and

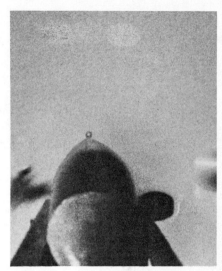

target the instant it appears, covers it and breaks it halfway to 8.

call for the target. The moment it appears, place the gun to your face and shoulder and move the bead of the barrel along the flight path at the same time, so you can cover the target with your bead. You should cover it at a point about halfway from the high house to Station 8. This is basically a single short, smooth movement that involves raising the gun along the flight of the target, placing it to the face, backing it up by the shoulder, and covering the target with the gun muzzle—all in one continuous movement.

It is imperative that you fire the moment you see the target covered with your front bead. You have to move your barrel fairly fast, but the movement must be smooth. You must continue your follow-through here, as at all other stations. The reason you break this target at a point about half- **145**

NO LEAD

X In ready position, gun points here   ▬ Location of target when gun is fired
✳ Where gun points at instant of fire   ▬ Path of the target
— Line of fire   -- Follow-through along target arc

way from the high house to Station 8 is that up to that midway mark you have the gun point and target under control, as well as your sight of the target. However, once the target passes that midpoint you will be forced to bend your knees, lean backward, and point the gun with your arms mechanically.

For the low house target, follow exactly the same principles, because it is exactly the same kind of shot. Here the correct foot position is the same as it was for Station 1. Facing the low house squarely, turn your body 45 degrees to the right, so that a line across your toes would make a 45° angle with a line from Station 8 to the low house.

With the knee bent and the gun down and out, place your bead on the line of flight the target will

With the foot position used for Station 1, the bead of barrel is placed 6 to 7 feet out along flight of target.

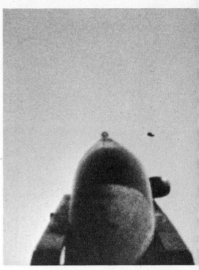

The camera-gun picks up this target as it leaves the trap house,

take from the low house and, as before, about 6 or 7 feet out from the trap mouth on this line. Note that this is the only low house target when the bead is not *under* the flight of the target. After making sure you are relaxed and physically alert, look at the trap mouth and call for the target. As it appears, begin to raise your gun to your face and, at the same time, begin to move the muzzle of your gun along the flight path of the target in a fast, smooth movement. Cover your target with the front sight at about the halfway point, fire immediately, and keep moving the muzzle of the gun as though you had not fired at all.

Points to Remember

Keep in mind the following at all stations:

It is imperative that a shooter should not be

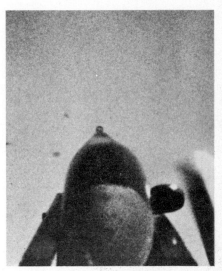

covers it, and target is broken by the time it gets halfway to 8.

tense, nor should he call for a target when his muscles are tightened. Point your gun at these targets just as if you were pointing your finger—in a fast, smooth, relaxed manner. And the moment you cover your target, fire and follow through.

Don't let the target get the jump on you. If you do, you will lose the graceful and relaxed swing that is essential in skeet.

Always shoot targets one at a time. Think of doubles simply as two singles.

Stations 3, 4 and 5 are the hardest. However, don't be lulled into a false sense of security on the easier targets. Each target is as important as the previous one.

It is better to give yourself too much lead than too little. Remember, it is not mandatory that you satisfy your desire to smoke every target.

149

IN THE FIELD

High 8 is like a dove, duck or quail situation in which one of these birds appears over a nearby hedge or row of trees.

Low 8 most resembles a duck or quail situation in which your presence has frightened or startled the bird. Both situations call for a fast, coordinated spot shot.

It has been mentioned earlier that clay targets travel at speeds ranging from 45 to 55 miles per hour under normal conditions, whereas the speeds of birds vary widely from one species to another. Moreover, there can be considerable variation in the speed of individual birds, depending on whether they are "cruising," "frightened," "gliding," etc. Consequently, in field shooting the hunter has to gauge by experience the leads he will need under the circumstances for particular species.

High 8 is the kind of field shot a hunter encounters where there is no time but to cover the bird and fire.

Low 8 is same, but with bird coming from lower cover. No lead is called for—only smooth, quick gun movement.

LEFT-HANDED SHOOTING

If a left-handed shooter will take all the instructions for a right-handed shooter and simply reverse them, he will then have everything exactly as it should be for him. The way of shooting each target at each station is exactly the same as it is for the right-handed shooter. The leads are the same, and so forth, but obviously the foot and body positions are different. They are, in fact, opposite to the right-hander's positions. Thus the left-hander's foot position on Station 1 is the same as the right-hander's on Station 7. Conversely, the left-hander's position on Station 7 takes the same angle as the right-hander's at Station 1. This same reversal holds for stations 2 and 6, and so on.

Station 1

A line across the toes extends directly to Station 8. The same foot position is kept for doubles here, as it will be for Stations 2, 6 and 7. This is the right-hander's stance at Station 7. Gun point for the high house is toward the target intersection point behind Station 8, with the muzzle tipped up at about a 30° angle and your gaze diverted upward about 15 degrees more than that.

Gun point for the low house is about two-thirds of the way from the target intersection point at 8 back to the low house.

Station 2

A line across the toes extends directly to Station 8. This is the right-hander's foot position at Station 6. Gun point for the high house is directly into the line from the high house to Station 8, but advanced about a yard toward 8. This is the same advance the right-handed shooter uses for Low 6.

Gun point for the low house is two-thirds of the way from 8 to the low house.

Stations 3-5

For the high house at each of these stations, a line across the toes should extend to a point 10 to 12 feet to the right of Station 8. This is the reverse of the right-hander's low house stance where the line runs 10 to 12 feet to the *left* of 8. Gun point for each house on these three stations is two-thirds of the way from Station 8 back toward either house.

For the low houses, a line across the toes reaches a point 8 to 9 feet out from the low house toward Station 8. This is the reverse of the right-hander's high house stance, when the line goes 8 or 9 feet out from that house.

Station 6

A line across the toes makes a 90° angle with the line from the low house to Station 8. This is like the right-hander at Station 2. Gun point for the high house is two-thirds of the way from Station 8 to that house.

Gun point for the low house is exactly parallel to the line across the toes. This is like the right-hander's point for High 2.

Station 7

Face Station 8 squarely and then turn your body 45 degrees to the left. A line across the toes then makes a 45° angle with a line from the low house to Station 8. This is the same angle taken by the right-hander at Station 1, except that he reverses the direction and turns to his right.

Gun point for the high house is two-thirds of the way from the target intersection point back to the high house. Gun point for the low house is toward the target intersection point.

Station 8

Foot position for the high house is the same as for Station 7. Gun point is 6 to 7 feet out from the trap mouth and on the line of flight of the target.

Foot position for the low house is the same as for Station 1. A line across the toes runs straight to the low house. Gun point is 6 to 7 feet out from the trap mouth and on the line of flight of the target.

Except for these foot positions all other factors are the same for the left-handed shooter as the right-hander. The southpaw should remember the same things, too: Keep the right knee slightly bent, hold the gun down and out, be relaxed, keep your bead on the line of flight of high house targets, but start with it under the line of flight of the low house targets except at Station 8. And always follow through.

153

AFTERWORD

I would like to leave with you a check list of the things you should keep in mind on each and every target, for you will need all of them for every shot. They are:

1) Correct foot position
2) Gun-point position
3) A relaxed but alert body
4) Bead on the line of flight for high house targets, but under it for low house targets
5) Proper lead for each target
6) Adjust lead for only a fraction of a second, then fire
7) Follow through every time

Most important of all, there is that psychological factor which will enable you to take all these things into account as you step up to the station. This is control and concentration, which enables you to put everything out of your mind and break just that next target. Believe me, that's the ball game!

If you can do this you can break 1000 straight targets. But it takes a lot of work and a lot of concentration. Like every other endeavor, however,

what you put into it will be proportional to the

pleasure you get out of it. At the conclusion of your shooting your enjoyment will come from the fact that you have done something you desired to do, something that came from your own efforts, your own willingness, and your own determination.

In conclusion, I want to be sure you understand that there are many systems of shooting. What I have described is the way *I* shoot. The success I have had personally is due to the factors and principles set out in this book. However, many whom I have instructed have had similar success and have won their own championships and national acclaim. It is this, more than my personal accomplishments, that has led me to think there might be something to say in a book.

I hope that you, too, have found information and helpful pointers in this book, something that may improve your shooting methods, your success at skeet and in the field, and hence something that may add to your shooting pleasure throughout your life.

Good luck.

Good shooting.

Happy hunting.

AND DON'T FORGET TO FOLLOW THROUGH.

FROM THE FRATERNITY

While preparing this book we wrote a number of prominent skeet shooters regarding Lee Braun's method of instruction. Below are excerpts from their responses.

"... Lee brushes aside many of the supposedly sophisticated fine points and hammers away on the basics ..."

Jay J. G. Schatz, Chicago, Ill.

"... I doubt if anyone before or since has helped so many become champions and All-Americans ..."

Gordon D. (Jack) Horner, San Francisco, Cal.

"I can think of some fine instructors over the years. But then there is one and only one D. Lee Braun. I always made it a point to look up Lee at any shoot I visited and generally found him back of a practice trap, sweating away with some beginner. His greatest love was helping people, especially youngsters, and he developed some of the greatest shots in the world. He has to be the greatest, in my book."

Jimmy Robinson, Skeet and Trapshooting Editor, *Sports Afield*

"... I was a mediocre skeet shooter with little hope of ever becoming anything else. Then Lee Braun took me under his wing and in one year [he] made me the Women's World Skeet Shooting Champion ..."

Thelma Anguish, Camarillo, Cal.

"Back in 1948 Lee took me aside and gave me one of the most valuable lessons in skeet. I had been gripping the gun, and my swing was jerky. Lee told me to relax, and I hit more targets ..."

Ed C. Scherer, Waukesha, Wis.

"... I arrived early for the World Championships at Dallas and asked Lee if he would work with me. He did, and I won the preliminary 410 event with a 98 x 100, the 410 World Championship with the identical score, and the Champion of Champions event ..."

Ben Di Iorio, Jr., Chatsworth, Cal.

"When Carola first began competitive shooting, we heard at once that there was a great teacher of the shotgun—Lee Braun. His reputation was so outstanding that Carola called Lee in Dallas and asked if he would work with her. He did, and moulded her into what she became ..."

Leon (and Carola) Mandel, Chicago, Ill.

"... He can not only teach you how to point a gun but how to think while you're doing it. He offers so much it becomes hard to define ..."

156

Clarine Menzel, Oshkosh, Wis.

". . . Without Lee, learning would have been tiring and uninteresting . . ."

Michael and Mark Pelkey, San Bernadino, Cal.

"Lee was everything a young boy could look up to and respect, for he understood and respected you . . ."

Barney Hilburn, Jr., Dallas, Tex.

". . . Thank goodness he is writing a book to give all shotgun shooters a chance to profit by his ability to teach . . . I always knew if I placed my feet and pointed the gun as he had taught me, I would break the target . . ."

Daphne Muchnic, Atchinson, Kan.

". . . There was a rhythm to the shooting movements he taught, a right feeling. And once I felt it I never forgot it . . ."

Jo Ann Wallis, Piedmont, Cal.

". . . The one thought I use so much from Lee's list of 'target-savers' is— be smooth . . ."

Marvin Hambrick, Lafayette, Cal.

". . . You could always recognize us Braun students by the relaxed way we went about our job of breaking targets."

Janice Mason, Lewes, Del.

". . . I attribute to Lee the building of my self-confidence, which it is necessary to have; the ability to shut other things from your mind; and the thought, as Lee would say, of 'one at a time—just break the next target, Son.'"

William T. Sesnon, III, Los Angeles, Cal.

". . . Mr. Braun believes if you tell yourself that you will break the target, you will do so. And he's right. It's all mental work, or at least 75% is. He's the only man in the world who knows how he breaks targets. This is what's so outstanding about him . . ."

Dianne R. Vermillion, Sherman Oaks, Cal.

"Lee Braun—a hard-head Dutchman—heart as big as all out of doors— patient and impatient—lovable. A great sport win or lose. Bad white wing shot. Very poor card player. The greatest clay target shot I have ever known. I salute you for your great contribution to the Shooting Game, both as a shooter and as a teacher."

Grant Ilseng, Houston, Tex. **157**

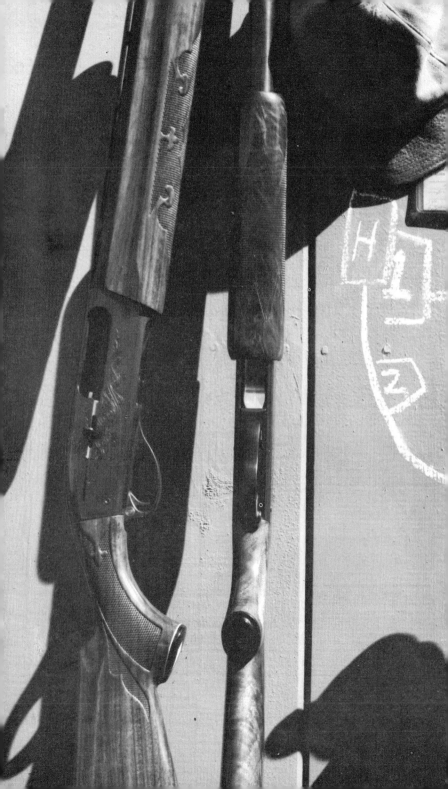

*Be sure to get your gun club or hunting group to schedule a showing
of the companion piece to this book, Remington's
16 mm. color and sound film, "Skeet Shooting with D. Lee Braun."
In the film, Lee personally discusses and demonstrates the proper
shooting of skeet targets and points up how this sport
will improve your field shooting. The film also contains an
important "first"—sequences, taken with a high-speed camera
mounted on a shotgun, that show the sight picture
you should have as you track, lead, break and follow through
on targets at the various skeet stations.
To order a print, write: Modern Talking Picture Service, Inc.
1212 Avenue of the Americas, New York, N. Y. 10036*

In the course of editing this film, Larry Madison, Jr., the producer's son, became interested in skeet, though he had done little shooting beforehand. While putting the film together, station by station, he began to try his hand on the skeet field. He did well on the stations he had already edited, having seen and heard Lee talk about how to shoot them. But he did poorly on the stations he had not yet come to. When he was finished with the editing, however, and heard Lee on all eight stations, he went out and broke his first 25 straight! It is presumed that if he now reads the book as well he will break 100 down the line.

To obtain an accurate sight picture of targets and leads as the shooter should see them at various stations on the skeet field, Remington engineers mounted a 12 gauge Model 1100 skeet gun on a heavy tripod and then attached Larry Madison's motion-picture camera to the 1100 so that the lens would sight right down the groove of the receiver. Running at high speed as it tracked clay targets, the camera gun recorded the sequences shown in stations 1, 2, 4 and 8.

---

*While this book was in preparation Lee Braun went to the Grand Amer
Trapshooting Tournament at Vandalia, Ohio, and won the profession
clay target championship with a 200 x 200 "at the tender age of 55,"
borrow a phrase from the author. "This achievement," says Lee,
"illustrates the power of concentration."*